AF680076

Defensible Healthcare Billing: Anesthesia Services

Documentation, Compliance, and Audit Strategy for Anesthesia

Linda Myrick CPC, CPC-I

Defensible Healthcare Billing Series

Copyright & Disclaimer

© 2026 Linda Myrick. All rights reserved.

No part of this publication may be reproduced or distributed in any form without prior written permission, except for brief excerpts used for review or instructional purposes.

This publication is part of the Defensible Healthcare Billing series and is not affiliated with, endorsed by, or sponsored by any governmental agency, professional association, certification body, payer entity, or code-set owner, including CMS, the American Medical Association, the American Society of Anesthesiologists, AAPC, or AHIMA. All trademarks referenced remain the property of their respective owners.

This text is intentionally written using a code-agnostic educational framework and does not reproduce or rely upon proprietary coding manuals, code sets, fee schedules, or valuation systems. Readers must consult current licensed coding resources, official payer policies, and applicable regulatory guidance when performing billing or reimbursement activities.

This publication is provided for educational purposes only and reflects interpretive analysis of publicly available guidance. It does not constitute legal, billing, or coding advice. Regulations and payer policies change frequently, and readers are responsible for verifying current requirements and applying independent professional judgment.

Table of Contents

Acronym Index

This index defines acronyms and abbreviated terms referenced throughout this publication. Definitions are provided for contextual understanding within billing, audit, documentation, and compliance discussions and are not intended as proprietary code instruction.

Regulatory, Governmental & Professional Organizations

ASA — American Society of Anesthesiologists
A professional medical organization that publishes clinical practice guidance and patient risk classification frameworks relevant to anesthesia care.

CMS — Centers for Medicare & Medicaid Services
The federal agency that administers Medicare, Medicaid, and related programs and issues national guidance on reimbursement, documentation, and compliance standards.

AMA — American Medical Association
A national physician organization that publishes medical education resources and maintains certain proprietary systems referenced descriptively in healthcare billing contexts.

NCCI — National Correct Coding Initiative
A CMS-developed program designed to promote consistent billing logic and prevent duplicate or inappropriate payment through nationally applied edit methodologies.

MACPAC — Medicaid and CHIP Payment and Access Commission
A nonpartisan federal advisory body that analyzes Medicaid and CHIP payment policy and access issues and advises Congress.

Audit, Review & Payer Oversight Terms

ABN — Advance Beneficiary Notice
A written notice informing a patient that a service may not be covered by Medicare and that the patient may be financially responsible if coverage is denied.

Pre-Payment Review
A payer review conducted before payment is issued to evaluate documentation, plausibility, or compliance.

Post-Payment Review
A payer review conducted after payment, often associated with higher financial risk and potential recoupment.

Determination
The formal outcome of an audit or review reflecting the payer's conclusion regarding payment, denial, adjustment, or recoupment.

Recoupment
The recovery of previously paid funds following an adverse audit determination.

Extrapolation
A methodology in which findings from a reviewed sample are projected across a larger population of claims.

Pattern Allegation
A payer assertion that identified findings represent systemic behavior rather than isolated error.

Healthcare Billing, Documentation & Compliance Concepts

Care Team Model
A structured approach to healthcare delivery in which responsibility for patient care may be shared among multiple qualified providers under defined roles and oversight requirements.

Complexity Indicator
A documented clinical factor that increases patient risk or management burden beyond baseline expectations and may influence reimbursement evaluation.

Concurrent Care
A situation in which a provider is responsible for more than one patient during overlapping periods of clinical service, subject to defined limits and availability requirements.

Continuous Clinical Responsibility
The uninterrupted period during which a provider maintains responsibility for managing a patient's care.

Documentation Alignment
Consistency across all records supporting a claim, ensuring clinical notes, time records, and provider roles corroborate one another.

Documentation as a Condition of Payment
The principle that reimbursement eligibility depends on clear, complete, and consistent documentation demonstrating required clinical and compliance criteria.

Medical Necessity
The requirement that healthcare services be reasonable, necessary, and appropriate for the patient's condition and supported by clinical documentation.

Procedure Mapping
The process of logically aligning anesthetic care with the surgical or diagnostic service performed based on clinical scope and physiologic demand.

Revenue Integrity
The discipline focused on ensuring healthcare services are billed accurately, compliantly, and consistently with documentation and payer requirements.

Time-Based Valuation
A reimbursement methodology in which payment is influenced by the documented duration of continuous clinical responsibility rather than a fixed service fee.

Compliance, Risk & Governance Concepts

Audit Readiness
The operational state in which documentation practices, internal controls, and workflows are consistently aligned with compliance expectations.

Containment
Immediate corrective action taken to halt further exposure when audit risk is identified.

Corrective Action
Targeted steps taken to address identified deficiencies, including education, process changes, or documentation improvement.

Governance Oversight
Leadership involvement in monitoring compliance trends, approving corrective action, and ensuring accountability.

Preventive Compliance
A proactive approach to compliance, focused on education, consistency, monitoring, and early risk identification.

Terms Intentionally Excluded

This publication intentionally omits proprietary code definitions, code ranges, valuation tables, and licensed manual content. Acronyms and terms related exclusively to proprietary coding systems are not defined in this index and should be referenced through current, licensed resources when required for operational use.

Preface

Anesthesia billing is a dynamic process, shaped by a series of interconnected decisions and documentation steps over time. Each claim represents ongoing clinical responsibility and must be thoroughly documented, logically organized, and prepared to withstand detailed review.

Reimbursement is determined by a combination of procedural scope, duration of care, provider roles, patient risk factors, documentation accuracy, and payer-specific methodologies. To construct defensible claims, professionals must understand how these elements interact and where misalignment commonly occurs during payer review.

This book is written for professionals who work with anesthesia services and want practical clarity. Designed for coders, auditors, clinicians, revenue integrity leaders, compliance professionals, and claims reviewers, focuses not only on how claims are constructed, but why they are evaluated the way they are and where they most frequently fail during review.

Rather than centering instruction on proprietary code sets, this text uses a code-agnostic framework to explain anesthesia billing concepts, audit risk, and compliance strategy. The emphasis is on decision-making, documentation alignment, and defensibility across payer environments, reflecting how claims are actually reviewed and challenged in real-world settings.

Note from the Author

The purpose of this series is to bridge the gap between technical billing knowledge and audit reality. The concepts presented here are drawn from recurring patterns seen in reviews, denials, appeals, and payer behavior, and are intended to support consistent, defensible decision-making rather than rote rule application.

If this book helps you approach anesthesia billing with greater clarity, confidence, and structure, and equips you to explain and defend your decisions under scrutiny, it has fulfilled its purpose.

Section 1 Coding, Documentation, & Reimbursement

Introduction

Foundations of Defensible Anesthesia Billing

Section I establishes the foundation for understanding how anesthesia services are translated into defensible reimbursement. Rather than focusing on isolated billing elements, this section explains how anesthesia claims are constructed as an integrated narrative, one that connects the procedure performed, the duration of continuous clinical responsibility, provider roles, patient risk, and supporting documentation.

Anesthesia reimbursement is not determined by how an anesthetic is delivered, but by how anesthetic care aligns with the procedure supported and the responsibilities assumed. Baseline valuation establishes a starting point, documented time converts clinical presence into measurable value, and role and risk indicators communicate both accountability and complexity. Because these elements are interdependent, a weakness in documentation or logic in any one area can undermine the entire claim.

The early chapters emphasize prevention as much as accuracy. Topics include how clinical responsibility begins and ends, how interruptions in care are managed, why multiple procedures map to a single primary anesthetic service, how bundled services are treated, and how different care models affect allowable reimbursement. Examples throughout this section reflect real-world billing disputes, situations where claims stall, are adjusted, denied, or revisited during later review.

By the end of Section I, the reader will be able to explain how an anesthesia claim is structured, translate documented clinical activity into defensible billing logic, and articulate, in clear, non-technical language, why a claim was reported the way it was. This foundation prepares the reader not only to submit accurate claims, but to support them confidently under audit and review.

Chapter 1 Coding: Why Anesthesia Is Different

Introduction

Anesthesia billing occupies a unique and often misunderstood position within healthcare reimbursement. Unlike most medical specialties, anesthesia services are not valued as discrete, one-time procedures. Instead, they are recognized as continuous clinical management that unfolds over time and across multiple phases of care.

This distinction shapes everything about how anesthesia services are documented, reviewed, and reimbursed. Payment is not determined by a single action, but by a combination of baseline complexity, elapsed time, patient risk, and provider responsibility. Each element must be independently supported, clearly documented, and logically consistent with the clinical record.

Understanding why anesthesia is different is essential before attempting to master billing rules, audit defense, or compliance strategy. Without this foundation, even technically accurate claims remain vulnerable to denial or recoupment.

Chapter Objectives

- Explain why anesthesia billing differs from traditional fee-for-service models
- Identify the core components that drive anesthesia reimbursement
- Understand anesthesia as a model of continuous clinical responsibility
- Recognize how documentation functions as a condition of payment
- Describe why anesthesia services are inherently high risk for audit review

Anesthesia as Continuous Clinical Management

Most healthcare services are billed as isolated encounters. A provider performs a service, documents it, and submits a claim tied to that single event. Anesthesia does not follow this model.

Anesthesia care is defined by ongoing responsibility, not by a moment in time. The anesthesia professional assumes continuous oversight of the patient's physiologic status, airway, consciousness, pain control, and vital functions throughout the perioperative period. This responsibility begins before anesthetic agents are administered and ends only when care is safely transferred to post-anesthesia personnel.

Because anesthesia spans preparation, induction, maintenance, emergence, and handoff, reimbursement must account for duration, not just activity. The longer and more complex the management, the greater the clinical workload and associated risk.

This is the fundamental reason anesthesia billing is calculated rather than fixed.

The Core Components of Anesthesia Reimbursement

While specific payment methodologies vary by payer, anesthesia reimbursement is generally built on four conceptual pillars:

1. **Baseline Complexity**
   A starting value that reflects the typical preparation, technical skill, and physiologic risk associated with the type of surgery performed.
2. **Duration of Care**
   The actual time during which the anesthesia provider maintains continuous attendance and active involvement in patient care.
3. **Modifying Factors**
   Additional clinical circumstances that increase risk or workload beyond what is considered typical, such as severe systemic disease, emergency conditions, or extraordinary physiologic management.
4. **Payment Multiplier**
   A payer specific dollar value applied to the total calculated units to determine final reimbursement.

Each component represents a different aspect of care and must be supported independently. An error or omission in any single element can invalidate the entire claim during audit review.

Why Time Matters in Anesthesia

Time is not incidental in anesthesia billing; it is foundational.

Anesthesia professionals are compensated not only for what they do, but for how long they remain responsible for the patient. This responsibility includes constant monitoring, rapid clinical decision-making, and readiness to intervene immediately if the patient's condition changes.

For this reason, anesthesia time is measured using actual clock minutes rather than estimates or averages. Start and stop times must reflect when anesthesia care truly began and when it definitively ended. Gaps in care, pauses in responsibility, or relief by another provider must be clearly documented and accounted for.

From an audit perspective, time documentation is one of the most heavily scrutinized elements of anesthesia claims. Patterned rounding, overlapping cases, or inconsistent timestamps frequently trigger denials and post-payment reviews.

The Anesthesia Care Team Model

Another feature that distinguishes anesthesia from many specialties is the care team model. Anesthesia services may be delivered by physicians, non-physician anesthesia providers, or a combination of both, depending on the practice structure and payer rules.

Reimbursement is influenced not only by what care was delivered, but by who delivered it, who was present, and how responsibility was shared. These distinctions are not administrative formalities; they are legal declarations that directly affect payment and compliance.

Documentation must clearly demonstrate:

- The role of each provider involved
- The level of physician participation
- The provider's availability during key portions of care
- Compliance with supervision or direction requirements when applicable

Failure to align documentation with the reported care model is one of the most common causes of payment downgrades and audit findings in anesthesia billing.

Documentation as a Condition of Payment

In anesthesia billing, documentation is not just supportive, it is essential for payment eligibility.

Payers require clear, affirmative evidence in the medical record that all necessary conditions were met, including:

- Continuous care
- Accurate time records
- Properly documented provider roles and compliance
- Clinical justification for any increased complexity

If any required element is missing, ambiguous, or inconsistent, payers typically assume the requirement was not met. This is why claims may be denied or adjusted even when appropriate care was provided. In compliance terms, "not documented" is equivalent to "not done."

Why Anesthesia Is a High Audit Specialty

Anesthesia claims are subject to frequent audits due to several factors:

- Variable, calculated payment structures
- Potential for inflated or inconsistent time documentation
- Complex compliance requirements in care team models
- Significant financial impact from minor documentation errors
- Automated payer systems that detect patterns and anomalies

Audits typically focus on patterns across multiple claims, such as repeated rounding, elevated complexity reporting, or discrepancies between documentation and reported care models. Early awareness of these audit risks enables practices to move from reactive corrections to proactive compliance strategies.

Case Study

When One Missing Element Collapses the Claim

Scenario

An anesthesia claim was submitted for a routine surgical procedure with no unusual intraoperative events. The record included a complete anesthesia record, documented start and end times, and a finalized operative report. At submission, the claim appeared structurally sound and passed initial processing.

Several months later, the claim was selected for post-payment review as part of a targeted audit focused on anesthesia services with above-average reimbursement relative to peer benchmarks.

Documentation Submitted

The organization provided the following records in response to the audit request:

Anesthesia Record (Excerpt):

"Patient brought to operating room. Monitoring initiated. Anesthesia care is provided throughout procedure. Patient transported to recovery in stable condition."

Time Documentation:

- Start of care documented at patient entry into the operating room
- End of care documented at patient transfer to recovery

Operative Report (Excerpt):

"Procedure performed without complication. Estimated blood loss minimal. Patient tolerated procedure well."

Post-Anesthesia Note (Excerpt):

"Patient awake, hemodynamically stable. No complications noted."

Notably, no documentation explicitly described provider responsibility, availability during care, or clinical oversight beyond general presence.

Audit Focus

The payer did not dispute:

- The procedure supported
- The duration of care as recorded
- The absence of complications

Instead, the audit findings centered on provider responsibility and role clarity.

Audit Finding (Excerpt):

"Documentation does not sufficiently demonstrate continuous provider responsibility throughout the reported service period. The record lacks detail regarding provider availability and oversight during the anesthetic course."

The reviewer concluded that while care was provided, the documentation did not clearly establish how responsibility was maintained for the entire reported period.

Outcome

Because provider responsibility is a foundational element of anesthesia billing, the payer determined that the overall billing structure was not fully supported by the documentation.

As a result:

- The claim was adjusted downward
- Time was partially disallowed
- The organization was advised that similar documentation patterns could result in expanded review

No allegation of inappropriate care was made. The adjustment was based entirely on documentation insufficiency, not clinical quality.

What Could Have Changed the Outcome

Even a brief clarification in the record could have altered the determination, such as:

"Anesthesia provider remained immediately available and clinically responsible for the patient throughout the procedure and until transfer of care."

This single statement would have directly addressed the audit concern without changing the care provided.

Strategic Insight

Anesthesia claims are evaluated as integrated structures. Accurate time and procedural support are not sufficient on their own. When provider responsibility is implied rather than clearly documented, reviewers may determine that the billing framework is incomplete—even when all other elements appear correct.

Why This Case Study Matters

This case illustrates a recurring audit theme: Claims most often fail not because care was inappropriate, but because key elements of responsibility and oversight were assumed rather than documented.

Anesthesia Claim Structure Map

Table: The Anatomy of a Defensible Anesthesia Claim

Element	What It Represents	Why It Matters in Review
Procedural Support	Service being anesthetically supported	Establishes scope and intent
Baseline Valuation	Starting complexity expectation	Sets reimbursement foundation
Time	Continuous clinical responsibility	Converts presence into value
Provider Role	Responsibility and availability	Determines allowable structure
Risk Indicators	Patient-specific complexity	Explains variation
Documentation Alignment	Consistency across records	Prevents misinterpretation

Chapter Summary

Anesthesia differs from other medical specialties by emphasizing ongoing clinical responsibility instead of isolated services. Reimbursement is based on baseline complexity, time, clinical modifiers, and payer-specific valuation, each requiring independent documentation. The care team model and increased audit scrutiny set anesthesia billing apart from traditional fee-for-service approaches. Understanding these foundational principles is crucial before progressing to detailed billing, audit response, or compliance strategies.

Chapter 2 Billing Structure & Reimbursement Methodologies

Introduction

Anesthesia billing is often described as "time-based," but that description alone is incomplete. While time is a central driver of reimbursement, anesthesia valuation depends on a structured framework that combines baseline complexity, duration of care, and documented clinical circumstances.

This chapter explains how anesthesia services are organized for billing purposes and how different reimbursement methodologies apply depending on the type of service delivered. Understanding these structures is critical not only for accurate payment, but also for audit defense. Many anesthesia denials and recoupments occur not because care was inappropriate, but because the reported methodology did not align with payer expectations.

Rather than focusing on proprietary code syntax, this chapter teaches the logic that governs anesthesia billing decisions, allowing readers to apply the concepts consistently across payers, years, and practice settings.

Chapter Objectives

- Describe how anesthesia services are structurally categorized for billing
- Distinguish between time-based and non-time-based reimbursement models
- Explain how baseline complexity influences reimbursement
- Identify common methodology mismatches that trigger denials
- Apply principles that support consistent, audit ready billing decisions

Structural Organization of Anesthesia Services

Anesthesia services are organized according to the type of procedure supported and the nature of anesthetic responsibility, not by how anesthesia is delivered. This organizational structure reflects anatomy, surgical scope, and anticipated physiologic stress rather than technique or duration.

From a billing perspective, anesthesia services fall into three structural categories:

1. **Primary Anesthesia Services**
   These represent the core anesthetic management associated with a surgical or diagnostic procedure. They establish the baseline complexity of care and form the foundation for reimbursement calculations.
2. **Supplemental Anesthesia Services**
   These reflect additional anesthetic work that extends beyond the baseline service, such as anesthetic management for staged procedures or extended operative involvement.
3. **Extraordinary Clinical Circumstances**
   These describe situations that significantly increase anesthetic risk or workload, such as emergency conditions or unusual physiologic management.

Each category serves a distinct purpose. Confusing or combining them improperly is a frequent source of billing error and audit exposure.

Baseline Complexity: The Starting Point

Every anesthesia service begins with an assumption of typical complexity based on the nature of the procedure being supported. This baseline reflects the preparation, skill, and physiologic management ordinarily required for that category of surgery.

Baseline complexity is not influenced by:

- How long does the case lasts
- Whether complications occur
- The individual provider's perception of difficulty

Instead, it is determined by the type and scope of the procedure itself. This distinction is critical. Inflating baseline complexity based on time or patient condition rather than procedural category is a common compliance error.

When multiple procedures are performed during a single anesthetic session, billing methodology recognizes the service as one continuous anesthetic, not multiple independent events. In these situations, the baseline complexity is determined by the procedure that represents the highest inherent anesthetic demand.

Time-Based Reimbursement Methodology

Most anesthesia services are reimbursed using a time-based methodology. This approach recognizes that anesthetic responsibility is continuous and that longer periods of management represent increased clinical workload.

Key principles of time-based reimbursement include:

- Time reflects actual clock minutes, not estimates
- Only periods of continuous anesthetic responsibility are included
- Gaps in care must be excluded
- Time is additive across the entire anesthetic session

Time-based billing requires precise documentation of when anesthetic care begins and ends. Even small inconsistencies can invalidate reported time during audit review.

Because time is a variable component of payment, it is also one of the most scrutinized elements. Patterned documentation, rounding habits, and overlapping responsibilities frequently trigger payer review.

Baseline Complexity vs. Base Units

One of the most persistent sources of confusion in anesthesia billing is the relationship between baseline complexity and base units. Conceptually, baseline complexity describes the expected intensity of anesthesia care for a given surgical procedure. Operationally, however, coders do not work with abstract concepts; they work with base units.

This disconnect often leads to misinterpretation at the very starting point of the anesthesia reimbursement formula.

Baseline complexity is not a measure of time. It does not increase or decrease based on how long anesthesia services are provided. Time is accounted for separately and independently within the reimbursement calculation.

Baseline complexity is not a reflection of patient illness or risk. Patient condition is addressed through physical status indicators and qualifying circumstances, not through the baseline value assigned to a procedure.

Baseline complexity is not a proxy for procedural difficulty, surgical stress, or provider effort beyond what is already assumed for the procedure itself.

Baseline complexity **is** procedure-driven only. It represents the inherent anesthesia workload expected for an average patient undergoing an average version of that specific procedure, absent unusual risk, extended duration, or exceptional circumstances. In billing terms, this expectation is translated into base units.

The critical mental shift is understanding that base units are not adjustable. They do not respond to documentation narratives, patient acuity, or operative challenges. Any increase in reimbursement must come from properly supported time, modifiers, or qualifying circumstances, not from reinterpretation of the baseline.

Non-Time-Based and Hybrid Methodologies

Not all anesthesia-related services are reimbursed based on elapsed time. Certain categories follow non-time-based or hybrid methodologies, depending on payer policy and service type.

Common examples include:

- Obstetric anesthetic services
- Specific monitoring or diagnostic services
- Postoperative pain management procedures
- Pre-anesthesia evaluations

In these cases, reimbursement may be based on:

- A fixed payment amount
- A capped or limited unit structure
- A per-service valuation independent of duration

Errors occur when time-based logic is incorrectly applied to services that are not paid by time. These mismatches frequently result in denials, payment delays, or post-payment adjustments.

Understanding which methodology applies is essential before determining how a service should be documented and reported.

Common Methodology Mismatches and Their Consequences

Many anesthesia billing errors stem from applying the wrong reimbursement logic rather than from incorrect documentation.

Frequent examples include:

- Reporting extended time for services paid on a flat or capped basis
- Combining multiple baseline services into a single calculation improperly
- Treating ancillary services as extensions of anesthetic time
- Applying time-based assumptions universally across all anesthesia encounters

These errors are particularly problematic because they often appear logical to the untrained eye. During audit review, however, they are evaluated against strict methodological expectations.

When the methodology is wrong, even perfect documentation cannot salvage the claim.

Multiple Procedures, One Anesthetic

A single anesthetic session may support multiple surgical procedures. From a billing standpoint, this does not create multiple anesthetic services.

Key principles include:

- Anesthesia is continuous across procedures performed in the same session
- Only one primary anesthetic service is recognized
- Baseline complexity reflects the highest inherent demand among the procedures
- Total time reflects the entire anesthetic period

Reporting anesthesia as fragmented or duplicative services is a common denial trigger. Payers expect anesthesia billing to mirror clinical reality: one provider (or team) maintaining responsibility for the patient throughout the operative encounter.

Audit Perspective: How Payers Evaluate Methodology

During audits, payers rarely start with documentation details. Their initial focus is whether the reported billing framework aligns logically with the clinical service provided.

Typical audit questions include:

- Does the methodology align with the type of service performed?
- Does the reported complexity match the procedural scope?
- Does the duration appear reasonable for the clinical scenario?
- Are multiple services logically combined or improperly separated?

When methodology fails these high-level tests, claims are flagged for deeper review, record requests, or systematic analysis across multiple encounters.

Practices that apply consistent, logical methodology experience fewer audits than those that rely on case-by-case interpretation.

Chapter Summary

Anesthesia billing relies on structured reimbursement methodologies that reflect baseline procedural complexity, duration of care, and documented clinical circumstances. While most anesthesia services are reimbursed using a time-based model, certain categories follow non-time-based or hybrid approaches. Applying the wrong methodology is a common source of denials and audit findings. Mastery of these structural principles allows anesthesia professionals to report services consistently, defensibly, and in alignment with payer expectations.

Chapter 3 Time, Documentation, and Concurrent Care

Introduction

Accurate time documentation is the backbone of anesthesia reimbursement. More than any other specialty, anesthesia relies on time to translate clinical responsibility into billable value. Because time directly affects payment, it is also the most heavily scrutinized element during audits.

Anesthesia time is not simply the length of a surgical procedure. It reflects the period during which the anesthesia provider maintains uninterrupted clinical responsibility for the patient. Errors in defining, documenting, or reporting this time routinely lead to denials, payment reductions, and post-payment recoupments.

This chapter explains how anesthesia time is defined, how it must be documented, and how concurrent care affects reimbursement eligibility. Rather than focusing on billing syntax, the chapter emphasizes defensible logic, clinical alignment, and audit expectations.

Chapter Objectives

- Define anesthesia time using audit-defensible principles
- Identify documentation practices that invalidate reported time
- Recognize when time must be excluded from billing
- Understand how concurrent care affects reimbursement
- Apply strategies to reduce time-based audit exposure

Defining Anesthesia Time

Anesthesia time represents the period during which the anesthesia provider is in constant attendance and actively engaged in managing the patient's anesthetic care.

From a practical standpoint, anesthesia time:

- Begins when the provider starts preparing the patient for anesthesia in the anesthetizing location
- Ends when care is transferred to qualified post-anesthesia personnel

Time does not include preparatory work performed outside the anesthetizing location, administrative tasks, or activities unrelated to active anesthetic management. Only periods of continuous clinical responsibility are eligible for inclusion.

Auditors evaluate time as a reflection of provider presence and accountability, not simply elapsed minutes.

Actual Clock Time vs. Estimated Time

One of the most common audit findings in anesthesia billing involves the use of estimated or rounded time rather than actual clock time.

Defensible time documentation must reflect:

- Specific start and stop times
- Consistency between anesthesia records and claim data
- Variability that aligns with real-world workflow

Patterns such as repeated full-hour cases or uniform time blocks across multiple encounters suggest estimation rather than documentation. Payers increasingly rely on algorithmic analysis to identify these patterns.

Even when total time appears clinically reasonable, patterned documentation alone may be sufficient to trigger audit review.

Discontinuous Time and the Exclusion Principle

Anesthesia time is not always continuous. Any period during which the anesthesia provider is not maintaining active responsibility must be excluded.

Examples of discontinuous time include:

- Surgical delays after induction during which anesthesia care is paused
- Periods when the provider leaves the patient and responsibility is transferred
- Extended breaks not covered by another anesthesia professional

If care is paused, time must stop. If care resumes, time may restart, provided the transition is clearly documented.

Failure to subtract discontinuous time is one of the most frequent causes of time-based overpayment findings during audits.

Time Conversion Is a Payer Rule, Not a Clinical Rule

Accurate anesthesia time documentation establishes clinical legitimacy, but it does not determine how time is paid. The conversion of documented minutes into payable time units is not a clinical standard, it is a payer-specific contractual rule.

The same documented anesthesia time may convert differently depending on whether a payer uses a 10-minute unit, a 15-minute unit, or another defined increment. In addition, payers vary in whether they apply rounding, truncation, or other proprietary conversion methodologies. These differences occur after clinical documentation is complete and outside the provider's control.

As a result, identical documented minutes do not guarantee identical payable units across payers.

Time conversion represents a significant contractual risk point in anesthesia billing. Applying an incorrect conversion methodology, even when time documentation is accurate, places the claim into the wrong payment model. From an audit perspective, this is not viewed as a minor calculation error, but as a failure to follow payer-specific reimbursement rules.

You must resist the temptation to "normalize" anesthesia time across payers. Standardizing time conversion for internal convenience can create systematic overpayment or underpayment, both of which carry compliance exposure. Each claim must be converted using the rules applicable to the specific payer, contract, and plan under which the service was billed.

Provider Presence and Key Phases of Care

Anesthesia care includes critical phases that carry heightened expectations for provider involvement. Documentation must demonstrate provider presence during these key periods.

While requirements vary by payer and care model, auditors consistently look for evidence that the provider:

- Initiated anesthetic care
- Remained available during maintenance
- Participated in the transition of care at the end of the anesthetic

When documentation does not clearly support provider presence, reported time may be reduced or disallowed entirely.

In audit review, ambiguity is interpreted unfavorably.

Concurrent Care and Its Impact on Time

Concurrency refers to situations in which a single provider is responsible for more than one patient during overlapping time periods. While concurrent care is permitted under defined circumstances, it carries strict documentation and availability requirements.

Concurrency is determined by overlapping anesthesia time, not by operating room assignment or scheduling templates.

Key principles include:

- There are limits to how many concurrent cases a provider may oversee
- Provider availability must be immediate and continuous
- Certain activities break availability and invalidate eligibility for higher reimbursement

Concurrency errors are often systemic, repeating across many claims, which increases the risk of extrapolated recoupments.

Time Legitimacy Framework

Table: Time That Counts vs Time That Does not

Time Segment	Included?	Audit Rationale
Patient preparation	Yes	Active clinical responsibility
Intraoperative management	Yes	Continuous monitoring
Temporary handoff (documented)	Yes	Responsibility maintained
Breaks without coverage	No	Responsibility interrupted
Post-transfer monitoring	No	Care transitioned

Activities That Break Availability

During concurrent care, certain activities remove the provider from immediate availability and therefore affect reimbursement eligibility.

Examples include:

- Performing lengthy procedures on another patient
- Leaving the anesthetizing area for extended periods

- Engaging in activities that prevent immediate response

Brief, incidental activities may be permitted depending on payer policy, but extended or procedural involvement typically invalidates concurrent care eligibility.

Documentation must reflect not only where the provider was, but also their ability to respond immediately if needed.

Documentation Alignment Across the Record

Anesthesia time documentation must be internally consistent across all components of the medical record, including:

- Anesthesia records
- Operative reports
- Post-anesthesia documentation
- Staffing schedules and call logs

Discrepancies between these sources are frequently identified during audits. When conflicts exist, payers tend to rely on the documentation that is least favorable to the provider.

Alignment across the record strengthens defensibility and reduces the likelihood of time-based challenges.

Common Time Documentation Errors

The following practices routinely lead to audit findings:

- Patterned rounding or uniform time blocks
- Missing or vague start and stop times
- Failure to subtract discontinuous time
- Overlapping time that exceeds allowable concurrency
- Documentation that conflicts with staffing records

These errors often appear minor in isolation but become significant when identified as patterns across multiple cases.

Audit Perspective: How Time Is Evaluated

During audits, time is evaluated as both an individual claim element and a pattern across claims.

Auditors assess:

- Whether reported time aligns with clinical reality
- Whether documentation supports continuous responsibility
- Whether concurrency limits were respected
- Whether patterns suggest systemic inflation or estimation

Time-based audits often escalate from record review to broader claim analysis. Preventive accuracy is far more effective than retrospective correction.

Case Study

Continuous Presence vs Continuous Responsibility

Scenario
An anesthesia provider documented start and end times that matched operating room entry and exit. During audit, the payer questioned time legitimacy due to overlapping cases.

Audit Focus
The reviewer did not dispute clock time. Instead, they evaluated whether the provider maintained continuous clinical responsibility during overlapping periods.

Outcome
Although start and stop times were technically accurate, the record did not clearly document availability or responsibility during concurrent periods. Time was reduced.

Strategic Insight
Time defensibility depends on documented responsibility, not timestamps alone. Concurrency must be explained, not implied.

Chapter Summary

Anesthesia must be documented using actual clock time supported by clear provider presence. Discontinuous periods must be excluded, and concurrent care carries strict availability requirements. Because time directly affects payment, it is heavily scrutinized during audits. Mastery of time documentation and concurrency principles is essential for compliant billing and effective audit defense.

Chapter 4 Provider Roles and Clinical Complexity Indicators

Introduction

Anesthesia billing is shaped not only by what care was delivered, but by who delivered it and under what level of responsibility. Provider role distinctions and patient complexity indicators directly influence reimbursement eligibility and audit exposure.

These elements are among the most frequently reviewed during payer audits because they affect both payment amount and compliance status. Errors in role designation or complexity reporting are rarely isolated. They tend to repeat across cases, making them attractive targets for pattern-based review and post-payment recoupment.

This chapter explains how provider roles and clinical complexity indicators function within anesthesia billing, why they matter, and how documentation must support their use in a defensible manner.

Chapter Objectives

- Distinguish between common anesthesia care models
- Understand how provider responsibility affects reimbursement
- Identify appropriate use of clinical complexity indicators
- Recognize documentation requirements that support complexity reporting
- Avoid common audit risks related to role and complexity misalignment

Anesthesia Care Models

Anesthesia services may be delivered under several care models, depending on practice structure, staffing, and payer rules. Each model carries different expectations for provider involvement, documentation, and reimbursement.

Common models include:

- Single-provider anesthesia care, in which one professional assumes full responsibility for the anesthetic

- Team-based anesthesia care, in which responsibility is shared between providers
- Supervisory or oversight models, in which one provider oversees multiple cases

These models are not interchangeable. The reported billing structure must reflect the actual clinical relationship documented in the medical record.

Why Provider Role Matters

Provider role declarations are not administrative labels. They are legal statements that communicate:

- Who was responsible for the anesthetic
- Who was present during key phases of care
- How oversight or direction was provided
- How payment should be allocated

Payers evaluate these declarations carefully. When documentation does not support the reported role, reimbursement is adjusted downward or denied.

Misalignment between reported role and documented activity is one of the most common causes of anesthesia claim downgrades.

Shared Responsibility and Team-Based Care

In team-based models, responsibility for anesthesia care is shared. While this approach allows efficient staffing and coverage, it introduces strict documentation requirements.

Documentation must demonstrate:

- Active involvement by each provider
- Appropriate oversight and availability
- Compliance with limits on concurrent care
- Clear delineation of responsibilities

When these elements are missing or unclear, payers may determine that higher-level reimbursement is not justified, regardless of the clinical skill involved.

Clinical Complexity Indicators

Clinical complexity indicators describe patient-specific or case-specific factors that increase anesthetic risk or workload beyond what is considered typical for the procedure.

These indicators may include:

- Severe systemic disease
- Significant physiologic instability
- Extreme age
- Emergency conditions
- Deliberate physiologic manipulation

Complexity indicators are not automatically assigned. They must be supported by clear clinical documentation that explains why the case required additional attention.

Patient Condition vs. Procedure Difficulty

A common compliance error is conflating patient condition with procedural difficulty.

Clinical complexity indicators reflect:

- The patient's underlying health status
- The physiologic challenges of managing anesthesia

They do not reflect:

- Surgical duration
- Technical difficulty of the operation
- Provider effort alone

For example, a lengthy procedure performed on a stable patient does not necessarily justify increased complexity designation. Conversely, a short procedure on a medically fragile patient may legitimately warrant it.

Auditors look for explicit clinical justification, not assumptions.

Modifiers as Legal Declarations (Operational Translation)

In anesthesia billing, modifiers are not descriptive add-ons or optional clarifications. They are formal declarations that define the payment model under which the claim will be adjudicated. When a modifier is applied, the provider is making an operational statement to the payer about how the service was delivered, who delivered it, under what conditions, and what level of reimbursement is being asserted.

From an audit and compliance perspective, modifiers function as binding signals. They instruct the payer's system, and later, human reviewers, how to interpret the claim. An incorrectly applied modifier does not simply adjust payment; it can place the entire claim into the wrong reimbursement framework.

Conceptual Role to Billing Modifier Category Mapping

Conceptual Role	**Billing Modifier Category**
Provider participation model	Medical direction / supervision modifiers
Patient risk stratification	Physical status (P-modifier) indicators
Service complexity or exception	Qualifying circumstance modifiers
Payment eligibility adjustment	Informational or payment-affecting modifiers
Documentation dependency	Modifiers requiring explicit record support
Audit risk elevation	Modifiers that trigger payer review

This mapping illustrates a critical principle: modifiers translate clinical and operational facts into reimbursement logic. They do not merely supplement a code—they define how the service is evaluated.

Modifier misuse is not a "minor error."
An incorrect modifier places the claim into the wrong payment model, which can result in overpayment, underpayment, recoupment exposure, or allegations of misrepresentation. Payers do not view modifier errors as cosmetic; they view them as structural.

Physical status (P) modifiers are not clinical adjectives.
They are risk multipliers that directly affect reimbursement and audit scrutiny. Reporting a higher

physical status asserts increased patient risk and provider workload—and requires documentation that independently supports that assertion. Unsupported risk escalation is a frequent audit trigger.

Documentation Requirements for Complexity Reporting

To support complexity indicators, documentation should:

- Identify the specific condition or circumstance
- Describe how it increased anesthetic risk or management burden
- Be consistent across the pre-anesthesia assessment, intraoperative record, and postoperative documentation

Generic statements or checklist selections without narrative support are frequently challenged during audits.

When documentation is vague, payers tend to default to the lowest allowable complexity level.

Emergency and Extraordinary Circumstances

Cases involving emergency conditions or extraordinary physiologic management receive heightened scrutiny.

To be considered defensible, documentation must clearly demonstrate:

- That immediate intervention was necessary
- That delay would have increased risk to life or limb
- That anesthetic management was altered as a result

Simply labeling a case as urgent or unplanned is insufficient. The record must explain why the situation met emergency criteria.

Emergency Designation: One of the Highest Recoupment Triggers

The emergency designation in anesthesia billing is not a descriptive label; it is a high-risk reimbursement assertion. When an anesthesia service is reported as emergent, the claim signals to the payer that immediate intervention was required to prevent serious harm. Because of its impact on payment and audit prioritization, emergency designation is one of the most frequently reviewed and recouped elements in anesthesia claims.

Coders must clearly distinguish true emergencies from situations that are merely urgent, inconvenient, or poorly scheduled.

Urgent does not equal emergent.

Time sensitivity alone does not establish an emergency. Many urgent procedures allow for reasonable clinical planning and stabilization and do not meet emergency criteria for anesthesia billing.

Scheduling failures do not create emergencies.

Cases delayed by operating room availability, staffing limitations, or administrative constraints do not become emergencies simply because time is compressed. Payers routinely deny emergency designations when urgency is driven by logistics rather than patient condition.

Documentation must demonstrate an immediate threat to life or limb.

Emergency anesthesia requires clear, contemporaneous documentation that delay would have resulted in serious risk of death, permanent injury, or loss of organ function. Absent this level of support, emergency designation is unlikely to withstand audit review.

Common Role and Complexity Errors

The following errors are commonly cited in audit findings:

- Reporting shared responsibility without documenting active involvement
- Assigning higher complexity without clinical justification
- Using template language that does not reflect the actual case
- Inconsistent role designation across providers
- Repeating the same complexity level across most cases

These patterns suggest systemic misuse rather than isolated mistakes.

Audit Perspective: How Payers Evaluate Roles and Complexity

During audits, payers evaluate role and complexity reporting by asking:

- Does the documentation support the level of responsibility reported?
- Are provider activities consistent with the declared care model?
- Do complexity indicators align with clinical reality?
- Are patterns consistent or artificially inflated?

When answers are unclear, claims are adjusted or recouped.

Chapter Summary

Provider roles and clinical complexity indicators play a critical role in anesthesia billing and compliance. Reimbursement depends on accurate representation of responsibility and defensible documentation of increased risk or workload. Misalignment between reported roles, complexity designations, and clinical documentation is a common source of audits and payment adjustments. Mastery of these principles supports compliant billing and effective audit defense.

Chapter 5 Bundled Services and the Anesthesia Care Package

Introduction

Bundling rules exist to prevent duplicate payment for services that are considered inherent to anesthesia care. In anesthesia billing, many tasks that may appear separately identifiable are already included in the primary anesthetic service and are not eligible for separate reimbursement.

Failure to understand bundling logic is one of the most common causes of denials, post-payment recoupments, and compliance findings. These errors frequently occur not because services were unnecessary, but because they were reported as separate when they were already included.

This chapter explains the concept of the anesthesia care package, how bundling is evaluated, and how to distinguish between included services and those that may qualify for separate consideration. Rather than focusing on billing syntax, the chapter emphasizes decision logic and audit defensibility.

Chapter Objectives

- Define the anesthesia care package
- Identify services that are inherently bundled into anesthesia care
- Distinguish between integral and distinct services
- Recognize situations that create unbundling risk
- Apply audit-focused reasoning to bundled service decisions

The Anesthesia Care Package

The anesthesia care package represents a global service, not a collection of individual tasks. It includes all routine activities necessary to safely deliver anesthesia before, during, and immediately after a procedure.

Bundled services are not excluded because they lack value. They are bundled because they are expected components of anesthesia care and are already reflected in baseline valuation.

The care package typically includes:

- Pre-anesthesia assessment related to the procedure
- Standard monitoring and physiologic surveillance
- Routine airway management
- Routine vascular access
- Medication administration that is inherent to anesthesia
- Immediate post-anesthesia stabilization and transfer of care

Attempting to separately report these elements is considered duplicate billing.

Integral vs. Distinct Services

Understanding bundling begins with distinguishing between integral and distinct services.

Integral services are required to safely perform anesthesia. They are inseparable from the anesthetic and are always included in the global service.

Distinct services are those that are:

- Performed for a separate clinical purpose
- Not required to deliver anesthesia itself
- Clearly documented as independent of anesthetic management

Only services that meet the definition of distinct may be considered for separate reporting, and only when payer policy permits it.

Why Bundling Errors Occur

Bundling errors often arise from reasonable but incorrect assumptions, such as:

- The service required additional skill.
- The service took extra time.
- The service involved specialized equipment.

None of these factors alone make a service separately reportable. The determining factor is whether the service was necessary to deliver anesthesia or performed for a separate clinical purpose.

Auditors focus on function, not effort.

Commonly Included Services

The following categories are almost always considered bundled when performed as part of anesthesia care:

- Routine airway placement and management
- Standard physiologic monitoring
- Peripheral vascular access for anesthesia delivery
- Medication preparation and administration
- Patient positioning and routine protection
- Routine emergence and immediate recovery monitoring

These services are expected in nearly every anesthetic and are therefore included in the global service.

Services That May Be Separately Considered

Some services may qualify for separate consideration only when specific conditions are met. These situations are narrow and highly scrutinized.

Examples include:

- Specialized monitoring performed for a distinct diagnostic purpose
- Vascular access placed for reasons unrelated to anesthesia delivery
- Postoperative pain interventions requested for pain control rather than anesthesia
- Diagnostic procedures requiring independent interpretation and reporting

In these cases, documentation must demonstrate:

- A clear clinical purpose separate from anesthesia
- Independent medical necessity
- Separation from anesthesia time and responsibility

Without this documentation, separate reporting is vulnerable to recoupment.

Bundling Decision Guide

Table: Is This Service Separately Defensible?

Question	Yes	No
Is the service inherent to anesthesia care?	Included	Continue
Is there documentation of unusual circumstance?	Continue	Included
Is it clinically distinct from routine care?	Defensible	Included

Case Study

The Service That Was not Separately Defensible

Scenario
Additional services were reported separately during anesthesia care, based on the belief that they exceeded routine expectations.

Audit Focus
The payer evaluated whether the reported services were inherent to standard anesthetic management or supported by distinct documentation demonstrating separate clinical necessity.

Outcome
The services were determined to be included in routine anesthesia care. The absence of documentation supporting unusual circumstances resulted in denial of the additional reporting.

Strategic Insight
Bundling is not a limitation—it is an expectation. Services that are not clearly documented as distinct are assumed to be included.

The Independent Documentation Principle

A key audit standard applied to potentially separate services is the independent documentation principle.

If the anesthesia record were removed entirely, the documentation for the additional service must still stand alone as a complete medical record. This includes:

- Clinical indication
- Procedure details
- Provider responsibility
- Outcome or interpretation

Services documented only within anesthesia grids or flow sheets are frequently recouped when billed separately.

Postoperative Pain Management Distinction

Postoperative pain interventions represent one of the most common bundling risk areas.

To be considered distinct from anesthesia:

- The intervention must be performed for postoperative pain control
- The request should originate from the surgical plan
- Time spent performing the intervention must be excluded from anesthesia time
- Documentation must clearly separate the intervention from anesthetic management

Failure to separate these elements is often interpreted as duplicate billing.

Audit Indicators of Improper Unbundling

Auditors look for patterns that suggest improper unbundling, including:

- Routine reporting of additional services on nearly every case
- Lack of separate documentation for ancillary procedures
- Inclusion of ancillary service time within anesthesia time
- Identical documentation language across multiple cases

These patterns are often used to justify expanded review or extrapolation.

Methodical Review: A Bundling Decision Framework

Before considering any service for separate reporting, apply the following logic:

- Was the service required to deliver anesthesia?
    - If yes, it is bundled.
- Was the service performed for a distinct clinical purpose?
    - If not, it is bundled.
- Is there independent documentation supporting the service?
    - If not, it is bundled.
- Was time clearly separated from anesthesia responsibility?
    - If not, it is bundled.

This conservative approach reduces audit exposure and promotes consistency.

Audit Perspective: How Payers Evaluate Bundling

Payers evaluate bundling by asking:

- Does the service add new clinical value beyond anesthesia delivery?
- Would anesthesia have been safely delivered without it?
- Is documentation sufficient to support separation?

If the answer to any of these questions is unclear, separate payment is unlikely.

Chapter Summary

The anesthesia care package includes all routine services required to safely deliver anesthesia. Attempting to separately report integral services creates significant audit risk. Only services performed for a distinct clinical purpose, supported by independent documentation and clearly separated from anesthesia responsibility, may qualify for separate consideration. Mastery of bundling logic is essential for compliant billing and audit defense.

Chapter 6 Procedure Mapping Logic and Revenue Integrity

Introduction

Accurate anesthesia billing depends on correctly linking anesthetic care to the surgical or diagnostic service it supports. This linkage, often referred to operationally as "procedure mapping," is one of the most consequential steps in anesthesia reimbursement.

When mapping logic is incorrect, the resulting errors are rarely isolated. They repeat systematically, affecting every occurrence of the same procedure and creating ongoing underpayment, overpayment, or audit exposure. For this reason, mapping errors are among the most financially significant risks in anesthesia revenue integrity.

This chapter explains how anesthesia services are logically aligned to supported procedures, why correct mapping matters, and how payers evaluate these decisions during audits. The focus is on decision-making principles, not proprietary mappings.

Chapter Objectives

- Explain the purpose of anesthesia procedure mapping
- Apply logic to align anesthesia services with supported procedures
- Distinguish between direct and judgment-based mapping scenarios
- Identify revenue and compliance risks associated with mapping errors
- Defend mapping decisions using operative documentation

What Procedure Mapping Accomplishes

Procedure mapping connects the anesthetic service to the clinical scope and physiologic demand of the procedure being performed. It establishes the baseline valuation of anesthesia care by answering a fundamental question:

What level of anesthetic management was reasonably required to support this procedure?

This determination is based on:

- Surgical intent
- Anatomic region
- Operative approach
- Expected physiologic stress

Mapping is not influenced by time, complications, or provider effort. Those elements are addressed elsewhere in the billing structure.

Why Mapping Errors Matter

Mapping errors have disproportionate impact because they affect baseline valuation, which applies to every occurrence of a procedure.

Consequences include:

- Chronic underpayment when mapping consistently understates anesthetic complexity
- Audit exposure when mapping overstates complexity without documentation support
- Claim denials or suspensions when payer logic detects misalignment
- Facility–professional mismatches that trigger automated edits

Because these errors can be repeated, they are easily identified through payer analytics.

Direct vs. Judgment-Based Mapping

Not all mapping decisions carry the same level of risk.

Direct mapping scenarios occur when the procedure clearly supports a single anesthetic category. These cases typically involve:

- Well-defined anatomy
- Standard operative approaches
- Minimal variability

Judgment-based mapping scenarios arise when:

- Multiple anesthetic categories may apply
- Surgical approach affects anesthetic demand
- Documentation determines the appropriate level

Judgment-based mapping requires careful review of the operative record and should never rely on defaults or templates.

The Role of the Operative Record

The operative record is the primary authority for anesthesia mapping decisions.

Critical elements include:

- Surgical approach (open, minimally invasive, endovascular, etc.)
- Anatomic structures involved
- Extent of operative field
- Whether the procedure remained within the planned scope

Mapping decisions made without reviewing the operative note are among the most common causes of audit findings.

One Anesthetic, One Mapping Decision

When multiple procedures are performed during a single anesthetic session, anesthesia billing recognizes one continuous anesthetic, not multiple independent services.

Key principles include:

- Only one baseline mapping applies
- The mapping should reflect the highest inherent anesthetic demand
- Baseline valuation is not additive across procedures

Fragmenting mapping across multiple procedures is a frequent cause of denial and recoupment.

Surgical Approach and Anesthetic Demand

The same surgical intent can involve different anesthetic demands depending on approach.

For example:

- Minimally invasive procedures may reduce physiologic stress
- Open procedures often require broader anesthetic management
- Endovascular approaches may alter monitoring and risk profiles

Mapping must reflect what was actually performed, not what was planned or scheduled.

Facility and Professional Alignment

Payers increasingly compare anesthesia billing logic with facility-reported services.

When facility documentation reflects one surgical approach and anesthesia billing reflects another, claims are often suspended or denied.

Alignment requires:

- Consistency between operative documentation and anesthesia mapping
- Awareness of facility reporting conventions
- Coordination between professional and facility billing teams

Misalignment is a common trigger for automated review.

Common Mapping Errors

The following errors are frequently cited in audits:

- Using generic mappings instead of procedure-specific logic
- Failing to update mapping practices after procedural changes
- Ignoring surgical approach documented in the operative note
- Selecting higher-complexity mappings without support
- Applying outdated mapping logic year after year

These errors are typically systemic rather than incidental.

Revenue Integrity Impact

Mapping errors affect revenue integrity in two distinct ways:

Undermapping

- Results in permanent underpayment
- Often goes unnoticed
- Accumulates significant financial loss over time

Overmapping

- Creates audit exposure
- Leads to denials and recoupments
- May trigger expanded review or extrapolation

Both outcomes undermine financial stability.

Defending Mapping Decisions During Audits

When mapping decisions are questioned, the strongest defense is operative documentation, not billing logic.

Effective audit defense includes:

- Quoting operative language that supports anesthetic demand
- Explaining why alternative mappings are inappropriate
- Demonstrating consistency across similar cases
- Showing awareness of procedural nuance

Appeals grounded in clinical documentation are far more successful than those based on reimbursement arguments.

Version Control and Ongoing Review

Procedural techniques evolve. Mapping logic must evolve with them.

Best practices include:

- Periodic review of high-volume procedures
- Monitoring changes in surgical technique
- Updating internal guidance proactively
- Training staff when procedural shifts occur

Failure to maintain version control is a common cause of outdated and inaccurate mapping.

Chapter Summary

Procedure mapping links anesthesia services to the surgical procedures they support and establishes baseline valuation. Errors in mapping create systemic revenue loss or audit risk. Accurate mapping depends on operative documentation, correct interpretation of surgical approach, and consistent application of logic. Mastery of mapping principles is essential for revenue integrity and audit defense.

Chapter 7 Professional and Facility Billing Alignment

Introduction

Anesthesia reimbursement depends not only on accurate documentation within a single claim, but on alignment between professional and facility billing. Payers routinely compare these two perspectives to confirm that the reported anesthesia service matches the surgical care delivered and the setting in which it occurred.

When professional and facility claims are inconsistent, payment delays, denials, and audits are common. These issues often arise not from clinical error, but from misaligned workflows, assumptions, or communication gaps between billing entities.

This chapter explains how professional and facility billing differ, why alignment matters, and how mismatches trigger payer scrutiny. Understanding these relationships is essential for preventing avoidable denials and protecting revenue integrity.

Chapter Objectives

- Distinguish between professional and facility billing roles
- Understand how payers evaluate claim alignment
- Identify common sources of professional–facility mismatches
- Apply strategies to synchronize documentation and billing logic
- Reduce audit risk related to claim inconsistency

Professional Billing: The Clinical Service Perspective

Professional anesthesia billing reflects the clinical service provided by the anesthesia professional. It communicates:

- Who provided anesthesia care
- How responsibility was structured
- The duration of anesthetic management
- Clinical circumstances that affected anesthetic complexity

Professional claims rely heavily on anesthesia records and provider documentation. Because these claims describe clinical responsibility, they are evaluated closely for consistency, provider presence, and compliance with care model requirements.

Errors in professional billing often relate to time documentation, provider role designation, or unsupported complexity reporting.

Facility Billing: The Encounter and Resource Perspective

Facility billing represents the institutional record of the surgical encounter. It reflects:

- The procedure performed
- The location of service
- Use of operating room or procedural space
- Institutional resources consumed

Facility claims establish the context in which anesthesia services occurred. They do not describe anesthetic management, but they define the procedural reality against which anesthesia billing is compared.

Payers frequently use facility billing as a reference point when evaluating anesthesia claims.

Why Alignment Matters

Professional and facility claims tell two sides of the same story. When those stories conflict, payers investigate.

Alignment confirms:

- That anesthesia services support the documented procedure
- That the anesthetic approach matches the surgical setting
- That reported complexity is reasonable for the encounter

Misalignment raises questions about accuracy, even when care was appropriate.

Common Sources of Claim Misalignment

Professional–facility mismatches often result from workflow disconnects rather than intent. Common causes include:

- Facility documentation reflecting a different surgical approach than assumed by anesthesia
- Professional billing based on scheduling information rather than operative records
- Updates to surgical technique not reflected in anesthesia billing practices
- Lack of communication between professional and facility billing teams

These mismatches are easily detected by payer analytics.

Location of Service and Its Implications

The setting in which anesthesia is provided influences how payers evaluate claims.

Different environments may involve:

- Different staffing models
- Different expectations for provider presence
- Different reimbursement methodologies

Professional billing must align with the documented location of service reported by the facility. When the two do not match, claims are frequently suspended or denied.

Synchronization of Documentation

Best practices include:

- Reviewing the final operative record before billing
- Ensuring anesthesia documentation reflects actual surgical approach
- Confirming consistency in start and end of the encounter
- Reconciling discrepancies before claim submission

Synchronization reduces the need for post-payment correction and audit defense.

Audit Perspective: How Payers Evaluate Alignment

During audits, payers commonly assess:

- Whether anesthesia services logically support the documented procedure
- Whether reported complexity aligns with procedural scope
- Whether professional billing assumptions match facility records
- Whether inconsistencies repeat across multiple encounters

When patterns of misalignment are identified, audits often expand beyond individual claims.

Facility–Professional Mismatch Case Pattern

A common audit scenario involves a facility documenting a minimally invasive procedure while professional anesthesia billing reflects a higher level of anesthetic demand typically associated with a more extensive approach.

Even when the anesthesia service was clinically appropriate, the discrepancy triggers review. Resolution requires demonstrating, through documentation, why the anesthetic management exceeded baseline expectations for the procedure as documented.

Absent that explanation, payment is frequently reduced.

Preventive Alignment Strategies

Organizations can reduce alignment risk by implementing:

- Shared review processes for high-risk procedures
- Clear communication channels between billing entities
- Periodic audits comparing professional and facility data
- Education focused on interpreting operative documentation

Preventive alignment is significantly more effective than reactive correction.

Chapter Summary

Professional anesthesia billing reflects clinical responsibility, while facility billing defines the procedural context. Payers routinely compare these perspectives to assess claim validity. Misalignment between professional and facility claims is a common cause of denials and audits. Consistent documentation, communication, and synchronization across billing entities are essential for compliant reimbursement and revenue protection.

Chapter 8 Diagnosis Logic and Medical Necessity in Anesthesia Services

Introduction

Every anesthesia service begins with a clinical question: Why was anesthesia required?
The answer to that question establishes medical necessity.

In anesthesia billing, medical necessity is not inferred from time, complexity, or outcome. It is established through diagnosis logic, the documented relationship between the patient's condition, the procedure performed, and the anesthetic management required to support it.

Claims that fail to demonstrate medical necessity are vulnerable to denial even when all other billing elements are technically correct. This chapter explains how diagnosis logic functions in anesthesia reimbursement, how payers evaluate necessity, and how documentation must support the clinical rationale for anesthetic care.

Chapter Objectives

- Explain how medical necessity is established for anesthesia services
- Understand the relationship between diagnosis, procedure, and anesthetic care
- Identify documentation gaps that weaken medical necessity
- Recognize audit risks related to diagnosis misalignment
- Apply defensible diagnosis logic in anesthesia billing and appeals

Medical Necessity as a Foundational Requirement

Medical necessity is a threshold requirement for payment. If necessity is not established, reimbursement may be denied regardless of how accurately other elements are reported.

For anesthesia services, necessity is typically demonstrated by:

- The presence of a condition requiring surgical or diagnostic intervention
- The need for anesthetic management to safely perform that intervention
- Documentation showing that anesthesia care was appropriate for the patient's condition and the procedure performed

Anesthesia does not exist independently. Its necessity flows from the clinical need for the supported procedure.

Diagnosis Logic vs. Code Selection

Diagnosis logic refers to clinical reasoning, not code assignment.

While formal diagnosis codes may be used for claims submission, auditors evaluate whether:

- The documented condition reasonably required the procedure
- The procedure reasonably required anesthesia
- The anesthetic management was appropriate given the patient's condition

When documentation supports this chain of reasoning, medical necessity is strong. When it does not, codes alone cannot salvage the claim.

The Diagnosis–Procedure–Anesthesia Relationship

Medical necessity in anesthesia is best understood as a three-part relationship:

1. Patient Condition
   The documented disease, injury, or physiologic state requiring intervention.
2. Procedure Performed
   The surgical or diagnostic service selected to address that condition.
3. Anesthetic Management
   The level of anesthetic care required to safely support the procedure for that patient.

Breaks in this chain weaken medical necessity.

For example, if the procedure does not logically address the documented condition, or if the anesthetic approach exceeds what the condition and procedure would reasonably require, the claim may be challenged.

Diagnosis Specificity and Clinical Clarity

Vague or generic diagnostic documentation is a common cause of anesthesia denials.

Effective documentation should:

- Identify the condition with sufficient clinical detail
- Explain relevant severity, acuity, or comorbidities
- Align with the procedural intent and scope

Statements such as "pain," "lesion," or "abnormal finding" without further context may be insufficient to support medical necessity, particularly when anesthesia services are questioned.

Auditors do not require exhaustive diagnostic detail, but they do require clarity.

Medical Necessity vs. Complexity

Medical necessity and complexity are related but distinct concepts.

Medical necessity answers:

Was anesthesia required at all for this patient and procedure?

Complexity addresses:

Did this case require additional anesthetic management beyond baseline?

A claim may meet medical necessity while failing to support elevated complexity. Confusing these concepts often leads to overstatement and audit exposure.

Special Considerations in Anesthesia Necessity

Certain scenarios receive heightened scrutiny:

- Procedures that may be performed with or without anesthesia
- Short or minimally invasive procedures
- Cases involving monitored care rather than full anesthetic management

In these situations, documentation should clearly explain:

- Why anesthesia was chosen
- Why lesser interventions were not sufficient
- How patient condition influenced anesthetic decision-making

Absent this explanation, necessity may be questioned.

Inpatient vs. Outpatient Context

The setting in which care is delivered influences how diagnosis logic is evaluated.

In inpatient environments, documentation often emphasizes:

- Severity of illness
- Physiologic instability
- Interaction with broader treatment plans

In outpatient settings, auditors may expect:

- Clear justification for anesthesia
- Alignment between procedure scope and anesthetic depth
- Absence of unnecessary escalation

Understanding context helps anticipate payer expectations.

Diagnosis Alignment Across the Record

Medical necessity must be consistent across all documentation sources, including:

- Pre-procedure assessments
- Operative reports
- Anesthesia records
- Post-procedure notes

Conflicting or incomplete narratives weaken necessity arguments. When discrepancies exist, payers typically rely on the documentation least favorable to the provider.

Common Diagnosis-Related Audit Findings

The following patterns frequently lead to denials or recoupments:

- Diagnoses that do not logically support the procedure
- Procedures that exceed what the documented condition would require
- Anesthetic management that appears excessive for the condition
- Repeated use of generic or non-specific diagnoses

- Inconsistencies between provider documentation

These findings often indicate systemic documentation issues rather than isolated errors.

Defending Medical Necessity in Appeals

When medical necessity is challenged, successful appeals focus on clinical reasoning, not billing mechanics.

Effective defense includes:

- Clarifying the patient's condition and risk profile
- Explaining why the procedure was appropriate
- Demonstrating why anesthesia care was required
- Aligning anesthetic decisions with documented clinical factors

Appeals grounded in patient-specific documentation are far more persuasive than those relying on general policy language.

Case Study

When the Procedure Was Valid, but the Narrative Was not

Scenario
Anesthesia was provided for a procedure that was clinically appropriate and covered. However, the documentation describing the patient's condition was minimal and nonspecific.

Audit Focus
The payer focused on whether the documentation explained why anesthesia was required for this patient, not whether the procedure itself was appropriate.

Outcome
The claim was denied due to insufficient demonstration of medical necessity. The procedure was not in question; the clinical rationale for anesthesia was.

Strategic Insight
Medical necessity depends on clinical explanation, not procedural validity alone. The "why" must be clearly documented.

Medical Necessity Alignment Model

Table: Medical Necessity Must Align Across All Three

Element	Must Answer
Patient Condition	Why is this patient different?
Procedure	What is being supported?
Anesthetic Care	Why was this level required?

Chapter Summary

Medical necessity is the foundation of anesthesia reimbursement. It is established through diagnosis logic that connects the patient's condition to the procedure performed and the anesthetic care required. Vague documentation, misalignment across records, and confusion between necessity and complexity are common audit risks. Mastery of diagnosis logic strengthens compliance, reduces denials, and supports effective appeals

Section I Summary

Coding, Documentation, and Reimbursement

Section I establishes the foundational logic of defensible anesthesia billing by explaining how anesthesia services are translated from clinical care into compliant reimbursement. Rather than treating billing elements as isolated rules, this section presents anesthesia claims as integrated structures that depend on alignment between procedure support, continuous clinical responsibility, documented time, provider roles, patient risk, and medical necessity.

Across Chapters 1 through 8, the reader is guided through the core components that shape anesthesia reimbursement. These chapters clarify why anesthesia is fundamentally different from other specialties, how reimbursement methodologies are constructed, and why time, provider presence, and documentation precision carry heightened audit significance. The section also addresses high-risk areas such as concurrency, care team models, bundled services, procedure mapping, professional–facility alignment, and diagnosis logic, all of which are frequent sources of denial and recoupment when misapplied.

A consistent theme throughout Section I is prevention. Many anesthesia audits and payment adjustments arise not from inappropriate care, but from structural misalignment or documentation gaps that weaken claim defensibility. By emphasizing logic, consistency, and audit perspective, this section equips readers to recognize risk early and correct it before claims are submitted or reviewed.

By the conclusion of Section I, the reader should be able to explain how an anesthesia claim is built, identify where claims are most vulnerable under review, and articulate—in clear, non-technical language—why a claim was reported the way it was. This foundation prepares the reader to move from claim construction to audit navigation, strategic defense, and preventive compliance, which are addressed in Section II.

Section II: From Audits, Denials, and Strategic Defense

Introduction

Audits are an expected reality of modern healthcare billing. They are not random, and they are rarely personal. In anesthesia services, audits occur frequently because reimbursement is variable, documentation-dependent, and highly suited to data-driven review. Understanding this reality is the first step toward responding effectively.

Section II is designed to demystify audits by explaining how they actually work. Rather than treating audits, denials, and appeals as isolated events, this section presents them as part of a predictable review cycle, one driven by payer analytics, pattern recognition, and risk assessment. When that cycle is understood, organizations can intervene early, respond strategically, and limit unnecessary escalation.

This section begins by explaining how audits originate and why anesthesia services attract scrutiny. It then examines common audit triggers, denial patterns, and payer behavior, emphasizing the importance of early recognition and disciplined response. As the section progresses, attention shifts to documentation requests, audit packaging, and determination analysis, areas where otherwise defensible claims often fail due to process missteps rather than clinical error.

Later chapters address appeals and advanced audit scenarios, including pattern allegations and extrapolation. These chapters focus on strategic defense, emphasizing clinical reasoning, documentation alignment, and governance involvement rather than technical argument alone. The section concludes by shifting from reaction to prevention, highlighting how audit readiness and preventive compliance reduce both audit frequency and severity over time.

This section is intended for professionals who are responsible not only for responding to audits, but for managing audit risk. Whether you are a coder, auditor, clinician, compliance leader, or revenue integrity professional, the chapters that follow provide a practical framework for navigating audits with confidence, and for building systems that make audits easier to withstand.

Audits may be unavoidable. Escalation is not. Section II provides the tools to recognize risk early, respond deliberately, and maintain control in an increasingly scrutinized reimbursement environment.

Chapter 9 The Anatomy of an Anesthesia Audit

Introduction

Anesthesia audits are driven by patterns, not by accusations. Typically, reviews are initiated when payer analytics detect statistical outliers, inconsistencies, or deviations from expected norms, rather than suspicions of fraud.

Recognizing how audits begin and progress enables organizations to identify risks early and take action before reviews escalate into recoupments or extrapolation. Viewing audits as isolated incidents can lead to missed opportunities for early intervention, whereas understanding them as part of a structured evaluation process leads to better outcomes.

This chapter explains why anesthesia services are frequently audited, how audit triggers develop, the types of audits payers use, and the predictable lifecycle that governs most reviews.

Chapter Objectives

- Explain why anesthesia services are particularly susceptible to data-driven audit review
- Identify structural characteristics of anesthesia billing that attract payer analytics
- Describe common audit triggers specific to anesthesia services
- Distinguish between statistical outliers and compliance violations
- Outline the progression from data outlier identification to formal audit review
- Differentiate between automated reviews, targeted medical record audits, and comprehensive post-payment audits
- Describe the predictable lifecycle of an anesthesia audit from initiation through appeal
- Recognize early warning signs that indicate potential audit escalation
- Analyze how documentation consistency influences audit scope and outcomes
- Apply strategic principles for responding appropriately at each stage of the audit lifecycle
- Evaluate how early organizational response affects payer perception and financial exposure
- Integrate audit awareness into proactive compliance monitoring and documentation practices

Why Anesthesia Is Audited Frequently

Anesthesia services are particularly well-suited to data-driven review. Several characteristics make anesthesia billing attractive to payer analytics:

- **Time-based reimbursement**
  Small changes in documented time can significantly affect payment, making time a high-value audit variable.
- **Variable provider care models**
  Differences in how responsibility and availability are structured introduce complexity and compliance risk.
- **Complexity indicators dependent on documentation**
  Increased payment often relies on narrative support rather than discrete events.
- **High financial impact from small documentation changes**
  Minor documentation inconsistencies can result in meaningful payment variation.
- **Repeatable billing patterns across cases**
  High case volume allows payers to analyze trends efficiently and at scale.

These factors do not imply wrongdoing. They create an environment where analytics can easily detect variance, prompting review.

Common Audit Triggers

Audit triggers are rarely tied to a single claim. They reflect trends observed over time.

Frequent triggers include:

- Unusual or clustered time patterns
- High or uniform use of complexity indicators
- Repeated documentation language across encounters
- Inconsistencies between professional and facility records
- Deviation from peer or historical benchmarks

Triggers are signals of perceived risk, not conclusions. They initiate inquiry rather than determine outcome.

From Outlier to Review

Most audits begin with identification of an outlier, something that falls outside expected ranges. Importantly, outliers may be clinically appropriate. However, from a payer perspective, outliers warrant verification.

When verification is limited to a small sample and documentation aligns with reported services, audits are often resolved quickly. When documentation is inconsistent or unclear, reviews tend to expand.

Understanding this progression helps organizations focus on early documentation alignment, where intervention is most effective.

Types of Anesthesia Audits

While terminology varies, anesthesia audits generally fall into three categories, each with distinct characteristics and risk profiles.

Automated or Algorithmic Reviews

These reviews rely on data analysis rather than manual chart review. They often trigger denials, suspensions, or documentation requests without human review of the record. Responses must be precise and restrained.

Targeted Medical Record Reviews

These audits involve focused review of selected claims and supporting documentation. They typically assess specific compliance elements such as time, provider presence, or documentation consistency.

Comprehensive Post-Payment Audits

These represent the highest level of scrutiny. They often involve extended timeframes, multiple claims, and financial recovery considerations. Strategy and containment become critical at this stage.

Each audit type requires a different response approach.

The Audit Lifecycle

Most audits follow a predictable sequence, regardless of payer or setting:

1. **Data Analysis**
   Identification of trends, outliers, or variance.

2. **Initial Claim Review**
   Limited review to assess whether further inquiry is warranted.
3. **Documentation Request**
   Targeted request designed to test specific compliance elements.
4. **Determination**
   Payer conclusion based on reviewed documentation.
5. **Recoupment or Closure**
   Financial recovery or resolution of findings.
6. **Appeal or Escalation**
   Opportunity for clarification, challenge, or further review.

Recognizing where an audit sits within this lifecycle informs appropriate response and resource allocation.

Audit Escalation Lifecycle

Table: Audit Stages and Organizational Risk

Stage	Payer Objective	Organizational Priority
Data Analysis	Identify outliers	Monitor patterns
Initial Review	Verify plausibility	Respond precisely
Documentation Request	Test compliance	Limit scope
Determination	Decide outcome	Assess risk
Recoupment	Recover funds	Contain
Appeal	Re-evaluate	Explain care

Case Study

How an Outlier Became an Audit

Scenario
A provider's anesthesia time consistently exceeded peer benchmarks for similar procedures.

Audit Focus
The payer identified this variance through data analysis and initiated a targeted review to verify documentation consistency.

Outcome
Although individual cases were defensible, inconsistent documentation language across records raised concerns, resulting in expanded review.

Strategic Insight
Outliers trigger audits. Consistency in documentation language is critical to preventing escalation.

Early Warning Signs

Certain indicators suggest that an audit may escalate if not addressed thoughtfully:

- Repeated requests for similar documentation
- Expansion of requested claim timeframes
- Requests for internal policies or training materials
- Language referencing patterns or trends

These signs warrant strategic review rather than routine processing.

Why Early Response Matters

The initial audit response often shapes payer perception. Early responses that are unfocused, excessive, or inconsistent may signal lack of internal control, encouraging broader review.

Conversely, disciplined early responses demonstrate:

- Awareness of compliance expectations
- Control over documentation and processes
- Willingness to address issues proactively

These signals influence how aggressively payers pursue further action.

Chapter Summary

Anesthesia audits originate from payer analytics that identify patterns and outliers. Because anesthesia billing is time-based, variable, and repeatable, it is particularly well-suited to data-driven review. Audits follow predictable pathways, beginning with data analysis and potentially escalating through documentation review, determination, and appeal. Organizations that recognize early warning signs and understand audit structure are better positioned to intervene early and manage risk effectively.

Chapter 10 Audit Triggers, Denials, and Payer Behavior

Introduction

Not all denials are equal. Some represent routine processing issues that can be resolved quickly, while others signal the beginning of deeper scrutiny. The ability to distinguish between these scenarios is critical. Early misinterpretation of payer intent often determines whether a review resolves efficiently or escalates into a prolonged audit.

Payers rarely approach claims randomly. Denials and reviews are shaped by data analysis, risk modeling, and prior provider behavior. Understanding how and why payers initiate reviews allows organizations to respond strategically rather than reactively.

This chapter explains common audit triggers, differentiates between pre-payment and post-payment review, and examines payer behavior patterns that influence escalation.

Chapter Objectives

- Differentiate between routine denials and denials that signal deeper payer scrutiny
- Explain how audit triggers develop from patterns, benchmarking, and risk modeling
- Identify common trigger categories that initiate anesthesia claim review
- Interpret denial characteristics as indicators of payer intent
- Distinguish between pre-payment and post-payment review and assess relative risk
- Describe strategic response principles appropriate to pre-payment reviews
- Evaluate the financial and compliance risks associated with post-payment audits
- Identify factors that commonly drive escalation from limited review to expanded audit
- Analyze payer behavior patterns, including benchmarking, replication analysis, and progressive escalation
- Assess how early response influences payer perception and audit scope
- Recognize when denials represent systemic concerns rather than isolated claim errors
- Explain why commercial payers frequently override CMS anesthesia guidance
- Identify common areas of commercial payer override, including modifier restrictions, time caps, and supervision downgrades
- Integrate payer-specific policy verification into anesthesia coding and compliance workflows
- Develop proactive strategies to reduce denial frequency and prevent audit escalation

How Audit Triggers Originate

Audit triggers are rarely tied to a single claim. Instead, they emerge from patterns, comparisons, and deviations identified through payer analytics.

Common trigger categories include:

- Unusual utilization patterns
- Documentation variability across similar services
- Time or complexity distributions outside expected ranges
- Inconsistencies between professional and facility data
- Rapid changes in billing behavior

These triggers do not necessarily indicate wrongdoing. They indicate perceived risk, which prompts payer review.

Understanding Denials as Signals

Denials are not merely payment decisions; they are signals of payer focus.

Some denials indicate:

- Administrative or technical issues
- Incomplete documentation submission
- Processing or formatting errors

Other denials suggest:

- Documentation sufficiency concerns
- Clinical necessity questions
- Structural or methodological misalignment

Recognizing the difference informs the appropriate response. Treating all denials as equal often leads to overreaction or under-response.

Denial Signal Decoder

Table: What This Denial Is Really Saying

Denial Characteristic	Likely Meaning	Best Response
Single claim	Routine issue	Correct
Repeated language	Pattern signal	Investigate
Pre-payment	Preventive	Clarify
Post-payment	Risk-based	Strategize

Pre-Payment Reviews

Pre-payment reviews occur before payment is issued and are designed to prevent improper reimbursement. While disruptive to cash flow, they often represent a lower-risk intervention.

Pre-payment reviews typically focus on:

- Documentation completeness
- Verification of reported elements
- Alignment between reported services and records

Because payment has not yet occurred, these reviews present an opportunity to correct issues without recoupment risk.

Strategic Response to Pre-Payment Reviews

Effective response to pre-payment review emphasizes:

- **Precision** – Submitting only what is requested
- **Completeness** – Ensuring required elements are present
- **Restraint** – Avoiding unnecessary documentation

Over-submission at this stage often converts manageable reviews into expanded inquiries.

Organizations that respond clearly and narrowly are more likely to see pre-payment reviews resolved quickly.

Post-Payment Reviews

Post-payment reviews carry significantly greater risk. At this stage, the payer has already issued payment and is evaluating whether recovery is warranted.

Post-payment audits may result in:

- Payment adjustments
- Recoupments
- Expanded sample reviews
- Extrapolated findings

Payers often escalate to post-payment review when they believe potential exposure extends beyond isolated claims.

Factors That Drive Escalation

Escalation from pre-payment to post-payment review commonly occurs when:

- The same issue appears repeatedly
- Prior review outcomes did not change behavior
- Financial impact is material
- Documentation inconsistencies persist

Escalation reflects a shift from claim-level concern to process-level evaluation.

Case Study

The Denial That Was not About the Denial

Scenario
A claim was denied for what appeared to be a minor documentation issue. The organization treated it as routine and resubmitted it without further review.

Audit Focus
The denial was part of a broader pattern analysis related to time reporting.

Outcome
Because the underlying concern was not addressed, the payer escalated to post-payment review of multiple claims.

Strategic Insight
Some denials are signals, not outcomes. Understanding payer intent determines whether a response resolves or escalates review.

Payer Behavior Patterns

While payer methodologies vary, certain behavior patterns are consistent across organizations.

Common payer strategies include:

- **Benchmark Comparison**
  Comparing provider behavior to peer norms, specialty averages, or historical baselines.

- **Pattern Replication Analysis**
  Identifying whether a questioned issue appears consistently across claims or time periods.
- **Progressive Escalation**
  Moving from limited review to broader audit when early interventions do not resolve perceived risk.

Understanding these patterns allows organizations to anticipate payer next steps and adjust response strategies accordingly.

Why Early Response Matters

The initial response to a denial or review often shapes the payer's perception of compliance maturity.

Early missteps may:

- Signal lack of internal control
- Encourage broader review
- Increase audit duration and scope

Conversely, disciplined early responses demonstrate:

- Awareness of compliance requirements
- Control over documentation processes
- Willingness to correct issues promptly

These signals influence how aggressively payers pursue further review.

Why Commercial Payers Frequently Override CMS Anesthesia Rules

A common and costly mistake in anesthesia coding is assuming that CMS rules represent a universal standard. While CMS guidance establishes a federal framework, commercial payers are not required to mirror CMS anesthesia policies and frequently apply their own contractual interpretations. When coders default to CMS logic without verifying payer-specific rules, claims are often adjudicated under an incorrect payment model.

Commercial payers routinely implement anesthesia reimbursement rules that override, narrow, or reinterpret CMS standards. These overrides are typically embedded in contracts, fee schedules, or internal payment logic rather than publicly visible policy documents, making them easy to miss and difficult to appeal after the fact.

Common areas where payer overrides occur include:

Disallowed or restricted modifiers
Commercial payers may deny or ignore certain modifiers that are otherwise recognized under CMS methodology. When a modifier is applied based on CMS logic alone, the payer may reprocess the claim without it or deny payment altogether.

Time caps and maximum payable units
Some commercial plans impose limits on payable anesthesia time, regardless of documented minutes. When these caps are exceeded, additional time units may be denied even if clinical documentation is complete and accurate.

Supervision and medical direction downgrades
Payers may apply stricter criteria for medical direction or supervision than CMS standards. In these cases, claims may be downcoded to a lower payment model despite documentation that would otherwise meet CMS requirements

Chapter Summary

Audit triggers and denials are driven by payer analysis of patterns and perceived risk. Pre-payment reviews present lower-risk opportunities for correction, while post-payment reviews signal greater concern and potential financial exposure. Payers use benchmarking, pattern analysis, and progressive escalation to guide review strategy. Early, disciplined response is essential to limiting scope and resolving reviews efficiently.

Chapter 11 Documentation Requests and Audit Packaging

Introduction

Documentation requests are not neutral. They are intentionally structured to test specific compliance elements, assess documentation consistency, and evaluate whether reported services can be substantiated under review.

How records are assembled and submitted often influences audit outcomes as much as the documentation itself. Clear, focused audit packaging supports reviewer understanding and limits unnecessary scrutiny. Disorganized or excessive submissions, by contrast, increase the likelihood of misinterpretation, expanded review, and adverse determinations.

This chapter explains how documentation requests should be interpreted, how audit packages should be assembled, and how strategic submission practices can materially reduce audit risk.

Chapter Objectives

- Explain why documentation requests are structured to test specific compliance elements
- Interpret documentation request language to identify underlying payer concerns
- Distinguish between routine record submission and strategic audit packaging
- Apply the principle of minimum necessary disclosure in audit response
- Evaluate the risks associated with over-submission and under-submission of records
- Identify common objectives of documentation requests, including verification of time, provider presence, and clinical complexity
- Recognize how record inconsistencies contribute to audit expansion
- Assemble audit packages that are organized, chronological, and clearly labeled
- Develop cover communication that orients reviewers without over-arguing
- Identify common audit packaging errors that increase risk exposure
- Conduct pre-submission reconciliation to ensure internal documentation consistency
- Analyze how audit packaging influences payer perception and determination outcomes
- Integrate audit packaging strategy into broader organizational risk management practices
- Apply lessons from case-based scenarios to prevent scope expansio

Understanding Documentation Requests

Audit documentation requests are designed to answer targeted questions. They are rarely broad by accident.

Common objectives include verifying:

- Provider presence and responsibility
- Accuracy and continuity of reported time
- Justification for increased clinical complexity
- Alignment between professional and facility documentation

Each requested record serves a purpose. Submitting documentation beyond what is requested can unintentionally introduce contradictions, highlight unrelated issues, or expand the scope of review.

Before assembling an audit package, it is critical to understand what the payer is testing.

Reading Between the Lines

The phrasing of a documentation request often provides insight into payer concerns.

For example:

- Requests emphasizing time suggest scrutiny of duration or continuity
- Requests for multiple provider records may indicate concurrency review
- Requests including facility documentation signal alignment evaluation

Understanding intent allows the response to be focused, precise, and proportionate.

The Principle of Minimum Necessary Disclosure

The principle of minimum necessary disclosure is foundational to effective audit response.

Only documentation explicitly requested should be submitted. Over-submission:

- Increases the chance of internal inconsistencies
- Introduces documentation unrelated to the audit issue
- Signals uncertainty or lack of control
- Expands reviewer opportunity to identify new concerns

Providing more documentation does not strengthen an audit response. It often weakens it.

Documentation Request Risk Matrix

Table: Documentation Submission Risk

Submission Type	Risk Level	Likely Outcome
Exact records requested	Low	Review closes
Slight over-submission	Moderate	Additional questions
Full chart dump	High	Scope expansion

Audit-Ready Record Assembly

An audit package should guide the reviewer through the clinical story logically and efficiently.

Effective audit packages are:

- **Organized**
  Records are grouped logically and presented in a consistent order.
- **Chronological**
  Documentation follows the sequence of care, from pre-service through post-service.
- **Clearly labeled**
  Each document is identified with a descriptive title that matches the request.
- **Clinically coherent**
  The narrative of care is easy to follow and internally consistent.

Well-assembled packages reduce reviewer effort and decrease the likelihood of misinterpretation.

Highlighting Key Elements Without Over-Explaining

While documentation should speak for itself, reviewers benefit from clarity.

Best practices include:

- Identifying where required elements appear in the record
- Using brief cover letters to orient the reviewer
- Avoiding commentary that argues rather than clarifies

The goal is to help the reviewer find relevant information quickly, not to persuade through volume or advocacy.

Common Audit Packaging Errors

Even well-documented claims can fail audit review due to poor packaging.

Frequent errors include:

- Submitting entire medical records when only portions were requested
- Mixing unrelated encounters or services
- Omitting key documents assumed to be "obvious"
- Providing conflicting versions of the same record
- Including internal notes or communications not intended for review

These mistakes often convert manageable reviews into adverse determinations.

Consistency Across Submitted Records

Audit reviewers compare documents within the submission for consistency.

Key areas of comparison include:

- Time documentation across records
- Provider roles and signatures
- Clinical descriptions of the service
- Transitions of care

Inconsistencies, even minor ones, are often interpreted unfavorably. Pre-submission reconciliation is essential.

Audit Packaging as Risk Management

Audit packaging is not a clerical task. It is a risk management function.

Organizations that treat packaging strategically:

- Limit scope creep
- Reduce review time
- Improve determination outcomes
- Preserve credibility with payers

Consistently poor packaging, on the other hand, can elevate an organization's risk profile and increase audit frequency.

Case Study

Over-Submission That Expanded Scope

Scenario
A documentation request asked for anesthesia records for one date of service. The organization submitted the entire hospital record.

Audit Focus
Reviewers identified inconsistencies between anesthesia notes and unrelated nursing documentation.

Outcome
The review expanded to multiple services and dates. What began as a narrow request escalated into a broader audit.

Strategic Insight
More documentation increases exposure. Minimum necessary disclosure protects defensibility.

Chapter Summary

Documentation requests are targeted tools used by payers to assess specific compliance elements. Effective audit response requires understanding the purpose of the request, adhering to the principle of minimum necessary disclosure, and assembling organized, coherent audit packages. Strategic presentation reduces audit scope, improves reviewer comprehension, and limits the risk of adverse determinations.

Chapter 12 Audit Findings, Determinations, and Recoupments

Introduction

Audit findings represent the payer's formal interpretation of compliance. They are not merely administrative outcomes, but decisions that reflect how documentation, billing logic, and clinical judgment were evaluated against payer expectations.

Understanding the type of determination issued is critical. Different determinations carry different levels of financial risk, operational impact, and appeal opportunity. Treating all findings the same is a common mistake that leads to unnecessary escalation, missed appeal deadlines, or avoidable financial loss.

This chapter explains how audit determinations are structured, what they signal about payer intent, and how organizations should respond strategically.

Chapter Objectives

- Explain how payers structure audit determinations and what those determinations signal about perceived compliance risk
- Distinguish between technical findings, denials, payment reductions, and recoupments
- Interpret determination letter language to identify whether concerns are technical, clinical, or systemic
- Evaluate the financial and operational risk associated with different types of findings
- Apply a structured framework to prioritize response based on risk level
- Identify when a finding suggests limited exposure versus broader organizational vulnerability
- Recognize escalation indicators, including sampling references and extrapolation methodology
- Differentiate between claim-specific recoupments and extrapolated financial recovery actions
- Assess when appeal is strategically appropriate and when corrective action without appeal may be preferable
- Preserve appeal rights through disciplined deadline tracking and procedural compliance
- Develop deliberate, evidence-based response strategies rather than reactive or emotional replies
- Conduct internal post-determination review to identify process, documentation, or education gaps
- Integrate audit findings into long-term compliance improvement efforts
- Use determination outcomes to strengthen internal controls and reduce future audit exposure

How Payers Frame Audit Determinations

Audit determinations are designed to answer two core questions:

1. Was the service compliant as reported?
2. If not, what level of corrective action is warranted?

Payers do not view findings as binary outcomes. Instead, they apply graduated determinations that reflect perceived severity, scope, and risk. The language used in a determination often provides important clues about whether the payer views the issue as technical, clinical, or systemic.

Careful reading of determination letters is essential before responding.

Types of Audit Determinations

While terminology varies, audit outcomes generally fall into several broad categories.

No Finding

A determination of no finding indicates that the reviewed claims were found to be compliant. While this outcome requires no further action, it should still be documented internally, as it establishes a favorable compliance record.

Technical Adjustment

Technical adjustments address minor issues that do not question the overall legitimacy of the service. These may involve formatting, documentation placement, or administrative inconsistencies. While often low-risk, repeated technical adjustments can signal process weaknesses.

Claim Denial

A claim denial reflects a determination that required criteria were not met. Denials may relate to documentation gaps, perceived lack of medical necessity, or misalignment with payer policy. Denials should always be evaluated for appeal potential.

Payment Reduction

Payment reductions occur when part of the reported service is deemed unsupported. These findings often relate to time, complexity, or provider role. Payment reductions frequently signal increased scrutiny of similar claims.

Recoupment

Recoupment represents the recovery of funds previously paid. This outcome indicates a higher level of payer concern and carries greater financial and compliance implications.

Each determination type requires a different response strategy.

Determination Response Matrix

Table: Responding Strategically to Findings

Determination	Risk Level	Best Action
No finding	None	Document
Technical adjustment	Low	Correct
Denial	Moderate	Evaluate
Payment reduction	Moderate–High	Appeal
Recoupment	High	Strategize

Understanding the Financial Implications

Not all adverse determinations present equal risk.

Low-risk findings may involve:

- Isolated claims
- Limited dollar impact
- No indication of broader concern

Higher-risk findings may involve:

- Multiple claims
- Repeated issues
- Language suggesting systemic noncompliance

Organizations should prioritize response based on risk level, not emotion or visibility.

Recoupments and Escalating Financial Exposure

Recoupments represent a shift from review to recovery. At this stage, payer focus extends beyond correction to financial remediation.

Recoupments may be:

- **Claim-specific**, affecting only the reviewed service
- **Pattern-based**, applying findings across similar claims
- **Extrapolated**, projecting sample findings to a larger population

Extrapolated recoupments represent the highest level of financial exposure and often indicate that the payer believes noncompliance is systemic.

What Recoupment Language Signals

Determination letters often contain language that signals escalation, such as:

- References to repeated findings
- Requests for policies or training materials
- Expanded record requests
- Discussion of sampling methodology

These signals should prompt immediate strategic review rather than routine appeal handling.

Case Study

When Accepting the Finding Was the Right Call

Scenario
A small number of claims were adjusted due to documentation inconsistencies. The financial impact was limited.

Audit Focus
The payer's language suggested isolated error rather than systemic concern.

Outcome
The organization chose not to appeal, corrected internal processes, and documented corrective action. No further review occurred.

Strategic Insight
Not every adverse determination should be appealed. Strategic restraint can preserve credibility and limit future scrutiny.

Responding to Audit Determinations

Initial response to an audit determination is critical. Early missteps can limit later options.

Immediate response priorities include:

- **Understanding the rationale**
  Identify exactly what the payer concluded and why.
- **Assessing scope**
  Determine whether the finding applies only to the reviewed claims or suggests broader exposure.
- **Preserving appeal rights**
  Track deadlines carefully and confirm submission requirements.

Responses should be deliberate and informed, not rushed, or reactive.

When to Appeal — and When Not To

Not every adverse determination should be appealed.

Appeal is most appropriate when:

- The determination is based on misinterpretation
- Documentation supports the service provided
- Financial or compliance impact is significant

In some cases, accepting a finding and correcting processes internally may be the most prudent course of action. Strategic restraint can preserve credibility and reduce future scrutiny.

Internal Evaluation After a Determination

Regardless of outcome, every determination should prompt internal review.

Key questions include:

- Was the finding isolated or indicative of a broader issue?
- Did internal controls fail to detect the issue earlier?
- Is documentation education or process correction needed?

Organizations that treat audit determinations as learning opportunities are better positioned to prevent recurrence.

Chapter Summary

Audit findings reflect payer interpretation of compliance and vary in severity from no finding to recoupment. Each determination carries different financial and strategic implications. Effective response requires understanding the rationale, assessing scope, preserving appeal rights, and choosing response strategies deliberately. Not all findings warrant the same reaction, and strategic evaluation is essential to long-term compliance success.

Chapter 13 Appeals Strategy and Effective Defense

Introduction

Successful appeals are built on clinical reasoning, not billing argument.
Payers do not reverse adverse determinations because a rule is cited; they reverse them when the documentation and narrative demonstrate that the care provided was reasonable, necessary, and appropriately supported.

An appeal must do more than challenge a conclusion. It must clearly explain why the care was appropriate for the patient, how the documentation supports that care, and where the original determination failed to account for clinical context. At this stage of review, precision matters more than volume, and clarity matters more than citation.

This chapter explains how effective appeals are structured, what distinguishes persuasive defenses from unsuccessful ones, and how to escalate strategically when initial efforts do not succeed.

Chapter Objectives

- Explain why successful appeals are driven by clinical reasoning rather than billing argument
- Distinguish an appeal as strategic communication versus claim resubmission
- Identify the core components of an effective appeal: issue identification, clinical narrative, documentation alignment, and logical rebuttal
- Translate payer determination language into a focused appeal objective
- Construct a concise, patient-specific clinical narrative that supports medical necessity and appropriate care
- Direct reviewers to specific documentation elements that substantiate the appeal argument
- Rebut adverse findings by clarifying misinterpretations, omissions, or inconsistent application of criteria
- Address common anesthesia-related audit findings, including provider presence, time legitimacy, clinical necessity, and documentation ambiguity
- Apply tone and framing strategies that improve credibility and reduce adversarial escalation
- Sequence appeals appropriately by matching depth and detail to the level of review
- Differentiate between weak appeal patterns (rule-citing, high volume, generic language) and strong appeal patterns (care-explaining, focused, patient-specific)
- Determine when escalation is appropriate and how to add value at higher review levels
- Reframe an appeal when initial arguments fail by shifting to clearer clinical context and decision points
- Apply lessons from case-based outcomes to strengthen future appeal performance and defensibility

Appeals as Strategic Communication

An appeal is not a resubmission of the claim. It is a targeted communication designed to address specific findings identified during review.

Effective appeals:

- Focus narrowly on the stated issue
- Respond directly to the payer's rationale
- Use patient-specific facts rather than generalized statements
- Present a coherent clinical narrative supported by the record

Appeals that attempt to re-argue the entire claim or overwhelm reviewers with unnecessary documentation are far less successful.

Anatomy of an Effective Appeal

While appeal formats vary, strong appeals consistently include four essential components.

Clear Issue Identification

The appeal should begin by identifying exactly what was denied or adjusted and why. Restating the payer's finding demonstrates understanding and keeps the response focused.

Concise Clinical Narrative

A brief narrative should explain the clinical scenario, emphasizing factors relevant to the determination. This narrative should connect the patient's condition, the care provided, and the clinical judgment exercised.

Documentation Alignment

The appeal must direct the reviewer to specific documentation that supports the narrative. Alignment across the record is critical. Contradictory or vague documentation undermines credibility.

Logical Rebuttal of Findings

The rebuttal should explain where the determination misinterpreted documentation, overlooked key facts, or applied criteria inconsistently. This is not an accusation; it is a clarification.

Volume does not equal strength. Well-reasoned appeals are often brief.

Appealing Common Anesthesia-Related Findings

While appeals principles are consistent across specialties, certain themes occur frequently in anesthesia-related determinations.

Effective appeals often focus on:

- **Provider responsibility and presence**
  Documenting uninterrupted clinical responsibility and appropriate provider availability in accordance with the applicable care model.
- **Time legitimacy**
  Explaining how documented time reflects continuous anesthetic management and excludes non-qualifying periods.
- **Clinical necessity**
  Clarifying why the patient's condition and the procedure required the level of anesthetic care provided.
- **Documentation clarity**
  Addressing ambiguities or omissions that led to misinterpretation during review.

Appeals grounded in patient-specific documentation consistently outperform generic responses or policy-driven arguments.

Tone and Framing Matter

Appeals should be professional, factual, and respectful. Adversarial language rarely improves outcomes.

Effective framing:

- Assumes good-faith review
- Clarifiers rather than confronts
- Focuses on clinical explanation
- Avoids emotional or defensive language

The goal is to guide the reviewer to a different conclusion, not to challenge their authority.

Timing and Sequencing of Appeals

Appeals should be submitted promptly, but not hastily. A rushed appeal that fails to address the core issue may limit later opportunities for review.

Best practices include:

- Reviewing the full determination before responding
- Identifying whether the issue is technical, clinical, or procedural
- Matching the appeal content to the level of review

Early appeals should be precise and restrained. More detailed argument may be reserved for later stages if necessary.

Appeal Effectiveness Model

Table: Why Appeals Succeed or Fail

Weak Appeals	Strong Appeals
Cite rules	Explain care
Generic language	Patient-specific
High volume	Focused
Defensive tone	Clarifying tone

Escalation Strategy

Not all appeals are resolved at the initial level. When an appeal stalls or is denied, escalation may be appropriate.

Escalation options can include:

- Supervisor or senior reviewer review
- Engagement with a medical director or clinical reviewer
- Independent or external review processes

Escalation should be deliberate, not automatic. Each step should add value, either through additional clinical context, clarification, or expert perspective.

Escalating without strengthening the argument often leads to the same outcome at a higher level.

Knowing When to Reframe the Argument

If an appeal is denied despite technically sound arguments, it may be necessary to reassess the approach.

Reframing may involve:

- Shifting focus from billing mechanics to clinical risk
- Clarifying documentation that was misunderstood
- Narrowing the issue to a specific decision point

Persistence alone is not a strategy. Adaptation is.

Case Study

Why the First Appeal Failed — and the Second Worked

Scenario
An initial appeal cited policy language and billing guidance but did not explain patient-specific clinical factors.

Audit Focus
The reviewer stated that the appeal did not address why the care was necessary for this patient.

Outcome
A second appeal reframed the argument around patient risk, procedural demands, and documented anesthetic management. The denial was overturned.

Strategic Insight
Appeals succeed when they explain care, not when they restate rules.

Chapter Summary

Effective appeals rely on clinical reasoning rather than billing argument. Strong appeals clearly identify the issue, present a concise clinical narrative, align documentation, and logically rebut audit findings. Tone, timing, and strategic escalation all influence outcomes. Appeals that focus on patient-specific facts and clear clinical explanation are the most successful.

Chapter 14 Advanced Audits, Allegations, and Extrapolation

Introduction

When audits progress from individual claim review to allegations of patterned behavior, financial and operational risk increases significantly. At this stage, the issue is no longer whether a single claim was processed correctly, but whether an organization's systems, processes, and decision logic are fundamentally flawed.

Pattern-based audits are designed to assess consistency over time. They are data-driven, comparative, and often retrospective. Early recognition of a pattern allegation, and an informed response, is critical to limiting scope, preventing escalation, and protecting revenue.

This chapter explains how pattern allegations arise, how extrapolation is applied, and how organizations can respond strategically when audits reach this advanced stage.

Chapter Objectives

- Differentiate between isolated claim error and alleged patterned noncompliance
- Explain how audits evolve from limited claim review to systemic evaluation
- Identify indicators that signal escalation from correction-focused review to pattern allegation
- Analyze how auditors assess frequency, consistency, and financial impact when alleging a pattern
- Describe how expanded sampling and broader timeframes increase organizational risk
- Explain the methodology and purpose of extrapolation in advanced audits
- Evaluate when extrapolation is most likely to be applied
- Assess financial exposure created by extrapolated findings
- Identify core defense components, including statistical review, clinical analysis, and process examination
- Develop strategies to challenge or narrow extrapolated recoupment demands
- Implement immediate containment measures to limit ongoing exposure
- Demonstrate evidence of internal controls, corrective action, and governance oversight
- Engage leadership appropriately during advanced audit stages
- Apply scope-narrowing strategies to reduce claim universe and timeframe exposure
- Integrate advanced audit response into long-term compliance infrastructure

From Claim Review to Pattern Allegation

Most audits begin narrowly. A small sample of claims is reviewed to determine whether further inquiry is warranted. When auditors identify recurring issues, the focus shifts from correction to systemic evaluation.

Pattern allegations typically emerge when auditors observe:

- Repeated documentation deficiencies
- Consistent application of unsupported billing logic
- Uniform use of higher-risk billing approaches
- Minimal variation across providers or encounters

At this point, the audit is no longer about isolated error. It is about whether the organization's practices demonstrate compliance integrity.

Pattern vs. Error: Why the Distinction Matters

The difference between an error and a pattern determines the auditor's next steps.

A single error suggests:

- Individual oversight
- Correctable mistake
- Limited financial exposure

A pattern suggests:

- Systemic failure
- Inadequate controls
- Ongoing financial risk

Auditors evaluating potential patterns typically assess:

- **Frequency** – How often does the issue occur?
- **Consistency** – Does the issue appear across providers or locations?
- **Financial impact** – What is the cumulative effect?

Once a pattern is alleged, the burden shifts to the organization to demonstrate that the issue is limited, explainable, and correctable.

How Pattern Allegations Escalate

Pattern allegations often lead to:

- Expanded sample sizes
- Broader timeframes
- Requests for policies and procedures
- Evaluation of internal controls

At this stage, payer focus extends beyond claims to governance and oversight. Auditors may evaluate whether the organization had reasonable processes in place to prevent the identified issue.

Failure to demonstrate internal control significantly weakens defense efforts.

Understanding Extrapolation

Extrapolation is the process by which audit findings from a reviewed sample are projected across a larger universe of claims. This methodology allows payers to calculate financial impact without reviewing every claim individually.

Extrapolation dramatically increases liability because:

- A small number of findings can result in large recoupment demands
- Financial exposure extends beyond the sampled claims
- Resolution timelines lengthen significantly

Extrapolation is most commonly applied when auditors conclude that identified errors are systematic rather than random.

When Extrapolation Is Most Likely

Auditors are more likely to apply extrapolation when:

- The same issue appears repeatedly
- Documentation deficiencies are consistent
- No evidence of internal monitoring exists
- Prior education or warnings were ineffective

Organizations that can demonstrate proactive compliance measures are less likely to face extrapolation.

Challenging Extrapolation: Core Defense Elements

Challenging extrapolation requires a multidisciplinary approach. Successful challenges often include one or more of the following components.

Statistical Review

Evaluating whether the sampling methodology was valid, representative, and appropriately applied.

Clinical Analysis

Demonstrating that alleged errors do not reflect clinical reality or were misinterpreted due to documentation nuance.

Process Examination

Showing that the issue resulted from limited circumstances rather than systemic failure and that corrective action was taken promptly.

Even when individual findings are upheld, narrowing or invalidating extrapolation can significantly reduce financial exposure.

Pattern Allegation Risk Scale

Table: When an Issue Becomes a Pattern

Indicator	Isolated	Emerging	Systemic
Frequency	Rare	Repeating	Consistent
Scope	Single case	Multiple cases	Broad
Payer language	Neutral	Cautionary	Escalating

Containment as a Strategic Priority

Once a pattern allegation is identified, containment becomes urgent. The goal is to prevent further exposure while the audit is underway.

Effective containment focuses on:

- Halting repeat behavior immediately
- Implementing interim controls
- Documenting corrective action
- Communicating changes clearly to staff

Auditors view timely containment as evidence of good faith and organizational maturity.

Narrowing Scope and Limiting Exposure

Organizations should actively work to:

- Limit the timeframe under review
- Reduce the claim universe subject to extrapolation
- Separate corrected claims from those under review

Delay or inaction increases the likelihood that auditors will assume continued noncompliance.

Governance and Leadership Involvement

Advanced audits require leadership engagement. Executive awareness and governance oversight signal seriousness and accountability.

Auditors often look for:

- Evidence of leadership response
- Formal corrective action plans
- Ongoing monitoring after intervention

Lack of leadership involvement is frequently cited in adverse determinations.

Case Study

How Delay Turned a Review Into Extrapolation

Scenario
An audit identified repeated documentation gaps. The organization delayed corrective action while preparing an appeal.

Audit Focus
The payer interpreted the delay as ongoing noncompliance.

Outcome
The audit expanded, and extrapolation was applied across a larger claim population.

Strategic Insight
Containment timing matters. Delay can convert manageable findings into high-risk exposure.

Chapter Summary

Advanced audits focus on identifying patterns rather than isolated errors. When patterns are alleged, financial exposure increases and extrapolation may be applied. Effective response requires early recognition, containment, statistical and clinical analysis, and strong governance involvement. Organizations that demonstrate proactive compliance and internal control are more successful in limiting scope and defending against extrapolated findings.

Chapter 15 Preventive Compliance and Audit Readiness

Introduction

The most effective audit strategy is prevention. Organizations that rely solely on reactive correction place themselves at a permanent disadvantage, responding to payer findings after financial exposure has already occurred.

Preventive compliance focuses on reducing the likelihood of audit selection, limiting escalation when reviews occur, and containing risk before it becomes systemic. In today's payer environment, where analytics-driven reviews and pattern analysis are standard, audit readiness is no longer optional. It is an operational requirement.

Preventive compliance does not eliminate audits, but it materially reduces their frequency, scope, and financial impact.

Chapter Objectives

- Explain why preventive compliance is more effective than reactive audit correction
- Identify organizational characteristics that increase the likelihood of repeated audit selection
- Describe how payer analytics and pattern analysis shape modern audit focus
- Design internal audit processes that detect trends and high-risk patterns early
- Distinguish between punitive auditing and proactive risk-control auditing
- Develop ongoing, role-specific documentation education strategies
- Connect documentation behavior to downstream audit and financial outcomes
- Establish role clarity and accountability within anesthesia documentation and billing workflows
- Implement consistency monitoring to reduce unintended billing variation
- Differentiate justified clinical variation from unexplained inconsistency
- Integrate governance oversight into compliance infrastructure
- Embed audit readiness into daily operational practice rather than episodic preparation
- Measure preventive compliance effectiveness using meaningful performance indicators
- Create feedback loops that convert audit findings into sustainable process improvement
- Build a preventive compliance framework that reduces audit frequency, limits escalation, and protects long-term revenue integrity

Why Preventive Compliance Matters Now

Modern audits rarely focus on isolated claims. Instead, payers evaluate patterns over time, comparing provider behavior to peer benchmarks, internal thresholds, and historical performance.

Common characteristics of organizations that attract repeated audits include:

- Inconsistent documentation practices
- Wide variation in billing approaches for similar cases
- Reliance on individual interpretation rather than standardized logic
- Lack of internal feedback loops

Preventive compliance addresses these vulnerabilities before payers identify them.

Core Elements of Preventive Compliance

An effective preventive compliance program is structured, intentional, and repeatable. While individual implementations vary, successful programs consistently include the following elements.

Internal Audits as a Risk-Control Tool

Internal audits serve as the primary mechanism for identifying risk before payers do. Their purpose is not fault-finding, but pattern detection and correction.

Effective internal audits:

- Review trends rather than isolated cases
- Focus on high-risk areas such as time, provider roles, complexity indicators, and medical necessity
- Use consistent criteria rather than subjective judgment
- Prioritize education and process improvement over punishment

When conducted regularly, internal audits provide early warning signals that allow organizations to correct course quietly and proactively.

Documentation Education as Continuous Training

One-time education is insufficient in a dynamic audit environment. Documentation education must be ongoing and role-specific.

Effective education programs:

- Explain why documentation matters, not just what is required
- Address common documentation gaps identified through internal audits
- Reinforce consistency across providers and teams
- Adapt to changes in payer focus and review behavior

Education that connects documentation choices to audit outcomes is significantly more effective than rule-based instruction alone.

Role Clarity and Accountability

Unclear provider roles create audit risk. Preventive compliance requires that every participant in the billing and documentation process understands:

- Their specific responsibilities
- How their actions affect downstream billing
- Where handoffs occur
- Who is accountable for final decisions

Role clarity reduces contradictory documentation, minimizes assumptions, and improves alignment across records.

Consistency Monitoring

From a payer perspective, inconsistency is often a stronger audit trigger than error.

Consistency monitoring focuses on:

- Whether similar cases are documented and billed similarly
- Whether complexity indicators are applied uniformly
- Whether time documentation follows the same logic across providers
- Whether exceptions are supported by clear clinical rationale

Consistency does not mean rigidity. It means that variation is intentional, justified, and documented.

Governance Oversight

Preventive compliance requires leadership involvement. Governance oversight ensures that compliance is embedded into organizational culture rather than treated as an afterthought.

Effective governance includes:

- Defined compliance leadership
- Regular review of audit trends and internal findings
- Clear escalation pathways for identified risk
- Authority to implement corrective action

Organizations with visible governance involvement experience fewer repeated audit findings and faster resolution when reviews occur.

Audit Readiness as an Operational Discipline

Audit readiness is not achieved through checklists or occasional preparation. It is the result of daily operational habits.

Audit-ready organizations:

- Document with clarity and intent
- Review high-risk activity proactively
- Maintain organized, accessible records
- Respond to payer inquiries promptly and strategically

When audit readiness is embedded into routine workflow, external audits become manageable events rather than disruptive crises.

Measuring Preventive Compliance Effectiveness

Preventive compliance should be evaluated using meaningful indicators, such as:

- Reduction in audit frequency
- Narrower audit scope
- Faster resolution timelines
- Fewer adverse determinations
- Improved confidence among staff

These outcomes reflect not only compliance success, but operational maturity.

Case Study

The Audit That Never Escalated

Scenario
A payer initiated a targeted review following data analysis.

Audit Focus
Documentation was consistent, internal audit processes were evident, and staff demonstrated awareness of compliance expectations.

Outcome
The review closed without adjustment or expansion.

Strategic Insight
Preventive compliance reduces escalation. Strong internal controls often stop audits before they gain momentum.

Preventive Compliance Loop

Table: Preventive Compliance in Practice

Activity	Outcome
Internal audits	Early detection
Education	Consistency
Monitoring	Reduced variance
Governance	Accountability
Readiness	Limited escalation

Chapter Summary

Preventive compliance is the foundation of effective audit readiness. Through internal audits, ongoing education, role clarity, consistency monitoring, and governance oversight, organizations can reduce audit frequency, limit escalation, and respond confidently when reviews occur. In an increasingly data-driven payer environment, preventive compliance is the most reliable strategy for protecting revenue and sustaining long-term operational stability.

Section II Summary

Audits are an expected reality in anesthesia services, driven by data analysis, pattern recognition, and payer risk assessment rather than isolated claim review. Understanding how audits originate, escalate, and resolve allows organizations to respond strategically rather than reactively.

Throughout this section, audits are presented as a structured review process with identifiable stages, each requiring a different level of response. From early denials and documentation requests to determinations, appeals, and advanced pattern allegations, effective outcomes depend on recognizing payer intent, maintaining documentation alignment, and responding with precision rather than volume.

By grounding audit response in clinical reasoning, disciplined documentation practices, and informed decision-making, organizations can reduce unnecessary escalation and limit financial exposure. Preventive compliance and audit readiness, when embedded into daily operations, further strengthen the ability to withstand scrutiny and sustain defensible billing practices over time.

Section II equips professionals with a practical framework for managing audit risk, protecting revenue integrity, and navigating payer review with confidence in an increasingly scrutinized reimbursement environment.

Appendix A Sample Audit and Appeal Communications

Editorial Note:
The following examples are provided to demonstrate structure, tone, and strategic reasoning. They are not templates and should be adapted to the specific facts, documentation, and payer correspondence associated with each review.

Sample Appeal Letter 1

Pre-Payment Documentation Request Response

Re: Documentation Request Dated [MM/DD/YYYY]
Patient/Account: [Identifier]
Service Date(s): [Date(s)]

This submission is provided in response to the documentation request referenced above. The enclosed records address the elements specified in the request and reflect the clinical care provided for the identified encounter.

Documentation is presented in chronological order for clarity and includes only those records relevant to the requested review. The information submitted demonstrates continuous clinical responsibility, appropriate provider involvement, and alignment between the care provided and the services reported.

Please contact us if additional clarification related to the requested elements is required.

Respectfully,
[Name / Title]

Sample Appeal Letter 2

Time Legitimacy Appeal

Re: Payment Adjustment for Reported Time
Patient/Account: [Identifier]

The reported time reflects continuous clinical responsibility from the initiation of patient preparation through the point at which the patient was stable for transfer from active care. No non-qualifying intervals are included.

Documentation across the anesthesia record, operative report, and recovery notes consistently supports this timeline. The anesthetic management required continuous monitoring, readiness to intervene, and ongoing clinical judgment throughout the documented period.

The reported time accurately represents the clinical services provided and is supported by the record as a whole.

Respectfully,
[Name / Title]

Sample Appeal Letter 3

Provider Responsibility and Presence

Re: Determination Questioning Provider Presence
Patient/Account: [Identifier]

The documentation supports continuous provider responsibility for the patient throughout the anesthetic course. Provider involvement and availability were maintained in accordance with the care model used, and the record reflects appropriate oversight and readiness to intervene as clinically required.

There is no indication of gaps in responsibility or absence from care. The determination appears to rely on an interpretation that does not account for the documented structure of care delivery.

We respectfully request reconsideration based on the documented provider role and clinical responsibilities reflected in the record.

Respectfully,
[Name / Title]

Sample Appeal Letter 4

Medical Necessity Clarification

Re: Denial Based on Medical Necessity
Patient/Account: [Identifier]

The anesthetic care provided was appropriate given the patient's condition, procedural requirements, and documented clinical risk factors. The record demonstrates why anesthetic management was necessary to safely support the procedure for this patient.

Clinical documentation reflects patient-specific considerations that influenced anesthetic planning and management. These factors are clearly described and align with the services provided.

We request reconsideration with attention to the documented clinical context supporting medical necessity.

Respectfully,
[Name / Title]

Sample Appeal Letter 5

Payment Reduction Rebuttal

Re: Partial Allowance / Payment Reduction
Patient/Account: [Identifier]

The payment reduction appears to be based on a misinterpretation of the documentation related to the reported service. The record supports the full scope of anesthetic management provided, including continuous responsibility and documented clinical involvement.

The determination does not appear to account for all relevant documentation elements when evaluating the reported service. When reviewed in full, the record supports the original submission.

We respectfully request adjustment based on the complete clinical documentation.

Respectfully,
[Name / Title]

Sample Appeal Letter 6

Pattern Allegation Response (Non-Extrapolated)

Re: Allegation of Patterned Billing
Review Period: [Date Range]

The findings identified do not reflect a systemic pattern, but rather a limited set of cases with patient-specific clinical characteristics. Internal review confirms that billing practices are applied consistently and supported by documentation across cases.

There is no evidence of uniform misapplication or process failure. Documentation and billing decisions are driven by clinical circumstances rather than standardized outcomes.

We request that the characterization of a pattern be reconsidered in light of the individualized nature of the reviewed cases.

Respectfully,
[Name / Title]

Sample Appeal Letter 7

Extrapolation Challenge (High-Level)

Re: Proposed Extrapolated Recoupment
Review Period: [Date Range]

We respectfully request reconsideration of the proposed extrapolation. The reviewed sample does not appear to represent the broader claim population, and the findings identified are not demonstrably systemic.

Differences in patient condition, procedural complexity, and documentation across the population limit the validity of projecting sample findings beyond the reviewed claims. Internal review and corrective action have been implemented where appropriate.

We request that recovery be limited to the specifically reviewed claims.

Respectfully,
[Name / Title]

Sample Appeal Letter 8

Good-Faith Corrective Action Letter

Re: Audit Findings Dated [MM/DD/YYYY]

We appreciate the opportunity to review the findings identified. In response, corrective action has been implemented to address documentation clarity and internal review processes.

Education has been provided to relevant staff, and additional monitoring has been initiated to ensure ongoing compliance. These actions were taken promptly and in good faith.

We remain committed to accurate, compliant billing practices and appreciate the opportunity to demonstrate continued improvement.

Respectfully,
[Name / Title]

Appendix B Audit & Appeal Checklists

Audit Intake & Triage Checklist

☐ Identify review type (pre- vs post-payment)

☐ Record deadlines and submission method

☐ Assess payer focus from request language

☐ Assign internal owner

Documentation Request Review Checklist

☐ Confirm exactly what is requested

☐ Exclude non-requested records

☐ Reconcile documentation for consistency

☐ Apply minimum necessary disclosure

Appeal Readiness Checklist

☐ Documentation supports care

☐ Issue is clinical vs technical

☐ Financial impact is material

☐ Appeal improves risk position

Pattern Allegation Response Checklist

☐ Determine if extrapolation is proposed

☐ Assess timeframe and claim universe

☐ Implement immediate containment

☐ Engage leadership oversight

Appendix C Clinical Concepts in Audit Review

This appendix defines clinical concepts that frequently influence how healthcare claims are evaluated during audits and payer reviews. The terms included here are not exhaustive clinical definitions. Instead, they reflect how clinical concepts are commonly interpreted in billing review, compliance analysis, and audit determination.

These concepts are included to support documentation clarity, audit readiness, and effective communication, not to provide clinical training.

Airway Management

Clinical management of a patient's airway during procedural care. In audit review, documentation related to airway management is often examined when higher complexity or increased patient risk is asserted.

Anesthetic Depth

A general descriptor of the degree to which a patient's consciousness and responsiveness are altered. Audit reviewers may consider anesthetic depth when evaluating whether the level of care provided was appropriate for the procedure and patient condition.

Clinical Stability

The patient's ability to maintain adequate physiologic function during care. Instability may justify increased monitoring, provider involvement, or extended clinical responsibility.

Clinical Narrative

A concise explanation of the patient's condition, the care provided, and the clinical reasoning that connects documentation to billing decisions. Strong clinical narratives reduce misinterpretation during audit review.

Comorbidity

The presence of additional medical conditions that may increase patient risk or management complexity. In audits, comorbidities must be clearly documented and clinically relevant to influence review outcomes.

Continuous Monitoring

Ongoing observation of patient status throughout care. Continuous monitoring supports the concept of continuous clinical responsibility and is frequently examined in time-based reviews.

Continuous Clinical Responsibility

The uninterrupted period during which a provider maintains responsibility for managing a patient's care. This concept underpins time-based valuation and is a frequent audit focus.

Emergence and Recovery

The phase during which anesthetic effects are reduced and patient stability is ensured following a procedure. Documentation during this phase may affect how the end of clinical responsibility is interpreted.

Physiologic Risk

The degree of risk posed by the patient's underlying condition, procedural demands, or response to care. Risk assessment is often implicit in audit review, even when not explicitly stated.

Procedural Invasiveness

A general characterization of the intensity or complexity of the supported procedure. Audit reviewers may consider procedural invasiveness when evaluating the reasonableness of reported services.

Provider Availability

The extent to which a provider is immediately available to intervene during care. Availability is a key concept in evaluating provider responsibility and concurrency.

Provider Presence

The documented participation of a provider in patient care. Presence may be direct or supervisory, depending on the care model, and must be clearly supported in the record.

Recovery Readiness

Clinical indicators that a patient is stable for transfer or discharge from active care. Recovery readiness may influence how clinical endpoints are interpreted during audit review.

Sedation Level

A general clinical descriptor of patient responsiveness and need for support. Sedation level may be scrutinized in audits when evaluating medical necessity or appropriateness of care.

Surgical Duration

The length of the operative or procedural component being supported. While distinct from anesthesia time, surgical duration may be referenced by auditors when assessing overall plausibility.

Time-Based Care

A care model in which valuation is influenced by the documented duration of continuous clinical responsibility rather than a fixed service fee.

Variability of Care

Differences in how similar cases are managed over time or across providers. In audit review, unexplained variability may be interpreted as compliance risk.

Purpose of This Appendix

These clinical concepts are included to help readers:

- Understand how clinical language is interpreted during audits
- Improve documentation clarity and alignment
- Anticipate payer questions during review
- Communicate clinical reasoning more effectively in audit and appeal contexts

Editorial Note

This appendix reflects common audit and compliance perspectives and is not intended to define clinical standards of care. Clinical decisions should always be guided by professional judgment and applicable clinical guidelines.

Glossary

Audit

A structured review conducted by a payer or oversight entity to evaluate whether billed services were reported, documented, and reimbursed appropriately based on applicable requirements.

Audit Lifecycle

The predictable progression of a review, typically moving from data analysis to claim review, documentation request, determination, recoupment or closure, and appeal or escalation.

Audit Packaging

The process of assembling, organizing, labeling, and submitting requested documentation in response to an audit or review in a manner that supports clarity and limits misinterpretation.

Audit Readiness

The operational state in which documentation practices, internal controls, and workflows are consistently aligned with compliance expectations, allowing organizations to respond effectively to audits at any time.

Baseline Valuation

The starting point for reimbursement determination reflects the inherent complexity of supporting a given procedure, before consideration of time, provider role, additional risk factors.

Billing Structure

The overall framework through which clinical services are translated into reimbursement, including valuation methodology, time reporting, provider responsibility, and documentation support.

Clinical Narrative

A concise explanation of the patient's condition, the care provided, and the clinical reasoning that connects documentation to billing decisions.

Clinical Reasoning

The documented thought process that explains why a service was appropriate for a specific patient, forming the foundation of medical necessity and defensibility.

Complexity Indicator

A documented clinical factor that increases patient risk or management burden beyond baseline expectations and influences how services are evaluated during review.

Concurrency

The management of responsibility for more than one patient during overlapping time periods, subject to defined limits and availability requirements.

Containment

Immediate corrective action taken during an audit to halt further exposure, prevent recurrence of identified issues, and demonstrate organizational control.

Continuous Clinical Responsibility

The uninterrupted period during which a provider maintains responsibility for managing a patient's care, forming the basis for time-based valuation.

Corrective Action

Targeted steps taken to address and identify deficiencies, including education, process changes, or documentation improvements.

Determination

The formal outcome of an audit or review, reflecting the payer's conclusion regarding compliance, payment adjustment, denial, or recoupment.

Documentation Alignment

Consistency across all records involved in a claim, ensuring that clinical notes, time records, provider roles, and narratives support one another.

Documentation as a Condition of Payment

The principle that reimbursement eligibility depends on the presence of clear, complete, and consistent documentation demonstrating required elements of care.

Extrapolation

A methodology in which findings from a reviewed sample are projected across a larger population of claims, significantly increasing financial exposure.

Financial Exposure

The potential monetary impact that is associated with audit findings, including denied payments, recoupments, or extrapolated recovery.

Governance Oversight

Leadership involvement in compliance processes, including monitoring audit trends, approving corrective actions, and ensuring accountability.

Internal Audit

A proactive review conducted by an organization to identify risk, evaluate documentation practices, and correct issues before payer review.

Medical Necessity

The requirement that services be reasonable, appropriate, and supported by the patient's condition and documented clinical rationale.

Minimum Necessary Disclosure

The practice of submitting only documentation specifically requested during an audit to avoid introducing unrelated issues or expanding review scope.

Pattern Allegation

A payer assertion that identified issues reflect systemic behavior rather than isolated error, often leading to expanded audits or extrapolation.

Payer Behavior

Observable patterns in how payers initiate, conduct, and escalate reviews based on perceived risk, data analysis, and prior outcomes.

Payer Intent

The underlying objective of a payer review, inferred from denial language, documentation requests, and audit scope.

Peer Benchmarking

The comparison of provider behavior to similar providers or historical norms to identify variance or potential risk.

Preventive Compliance

A proactive approach to compliance that focuses on education, consistency, and internal controls to reduce audit frequency and severity.

Recoupment

The recovery of previously paid funds following an audit determination.

Revenue Integrity

The discipline focused on ensuring that services are billed accurately, compliantly, and consistently with documentation and payer expectations.

Risk Assessment

The evaluation of potential compliance and financial exposure that is associated with billing practices or audit findings.

Scope Expansion

An increase in the timeframe, number of claims, or issues reviewed during an audit, often triggered by identified patterns or inconsistencies.

Strategic Appeal

A targeted response to an adverse determination that focuses on clinical reasoning, documentation alignment, and clarification of payer misinterpretation.

Time-Based Valuation

A reimbursement approach in which payment is influenced by the documented duration of continuous clinical responsibility rather than a fixed fee.

Utilization Pattern

The observable distribution of services over time may trigger payer review when it deviates from expected norms.

Index

B

C

D

E

P

R

T

U

Acknowledgments

This series reflects decades of work across the full spectrum of healthcare reimbursement, including professional and facility billing, auditing, compliance, and payer-side review and adjudication. My perspective has been shaped not only by supporting management, providers, and billing teams, but also by direct experience on the insurance side, reviewing claims, evaluating documentation, interpreting policy, and participating in audit and appeal decision-making.

Working within payer environments provided critical insight into how claims are actually evaluated, how audit focus is determined, and how decisions are made when documentation is incomplete, inconsistent, or unclear. That experience fundamentally influenced the Defensible Healthcare Billing framework. This series is intentionally written to explain not just how claims are submitted, but how they are reviewed, challenged, and ultimately judged under scrutiny.

I am grateful to the many professionals, coders, auditors, clinicians, compliance leaders, revenue integrity teams, and payer colleagues, whose real-world challenges, questions, and discussions helped refine the practical approach reflected in these books. Every audit reviewed, appeal evaluated, and policy debated contributed to the emphasis on judgment, structure, and defensibility that runs throughout the series.

A Personal Note

This work would not exist without the steady support of my husband, Gary Myrick.

For more than 35 years, Gary has stood beside me with patience, encouragement, and understanding, fully aware that I am both a workaholic and an education enthusiast. He supported long hours, endless research, constant learning, and the drive to always understand things more deeply and explain them more clearly.

His belief in my work never wavered, even when it meant sacrificing time, quiet, or routine. This series is as much a reflection of that support as it is of my professional journey. For that, and for everything else, I am profoundly grateful.

About the Author

Linda Myrick, CPC, CPC-I is a healthcare billing, auditing, and compliance expert with extensive experience across professional and facility reimbursement, payer audits, and complex claim appeals. Her work has focused on high-risk, documentation-dependent services where billing accuracy, clinical alignment, and audit defensibility are critical.

Throughout her career, Linda has worked closely with coding teams, clinicians, revenue integrity departments, and compliance leaders to identify risk, resolve audit findings, and implement defensible billing practices. Her expertise spans payer review processes, documentation standards, audit escalation, and appeal strategy, with particular emphasis on translating regulatory guidance into practical, real-world application.

Linda is known for her ability to explain how healthcare claims are evaluated under scrutiny, not just how they are submitted. Rather than emphasizing memorization of rules or reliance on proprietary code sets, her work focuses on clinical reasoning, documentation alignment, and consistent decision-making that withstands audit and payer review.

The Defensible Healthcare Billing series reflects this approach. Each volume is designed to help professionals understand how billing decisions are interpreted, challenged, and defended in modern reimbursement environments. Linda's goal is to equip coders, auditors, clinicians, and compliance professionals with the judgment and structure needed to manage risk confidently and sustainably across medical specialties.

This page intentionally left blank